ROUTLEDGE LIBRARY EDITIONS: LIBRARY AND INFORMATION SCIENCE

Volume 76

REFERENCE SERVICES IN ARCHIVES

REFERENCE SERVICES IN ARCHIVES

Edited by
LUCILLE WHALEN

LONDON AND NEW YORK

First published in 1986 by The Haworth Press, Inc.

This edition first published in 2020
by Routledge
2 Park Square, Milton Park, Abingdon, Oxon OX14 4RN

and by Routledge
52 Vanderbilt Avenue, New York, NY 10017

Routledge is an imprint of the Taylor & Francis Group, an informa business

© 1986 The Haworth Press, Inc.

All rights reserved. No part of this book may be reprinted or reproduced or utilised in any form or by any electronic, mechanical, or other means, now known or hereafter invented, including photocopying and recording, or in any information storage or retrieval system, without permission in writing from the publishers.

Trademark notice: Product or corporate names may be trademarks or registered trademarks, and are used only for identification and explanation without intent to infringe.

British Library Cataloguing in Publication Data
A catalogue record for this book is available from the British Library

ISBN: 978-0-367-34616-4 (Set)
ISBN: 978-0-429-34352-0 (Set) (ebk)
ISBN: 978-0-367-37204-0 (Volume 76) (hbk)
ISBN: 978-0-367-37211-8 (Volume 76) (pbk)
ISBN: 978-0-429-35305-5 (Volume 76) (ebk)

Publisher's Note
The publisher has gone to great lengths to ensure the quality of this reprint but points out that some imperfections in the original copies may be apparent.

Disclaimer
The publisher has made every effort to trace copyright holders and would welcome correspondence from those they have been unable to trace.

Reference Services in Archives

Lucille Whalen
Editor

The Haworth Press
New York • London

Reference Services in Archives has also been published as *The Reference Librarian,* Number 13, Fall 1985/Winter 1985-86.

© 1986 by The Haworth Press, Inc. All rights reserved. No part of this book may be reproduced or utilized in any form or by any means, electronic or mechanical, including photocopying, microfilm and recording, or by any information storage and retrieval system, without permission in writing from the publisher. Printed in the United States of America.

The Haworth Press, Inc., 28 East 22 Street, New York, NY 10010-6194
EUROSPAN/Haworth, 3 Henrietta Street, London WC2E 8LU England

Library of Congress Cataloging in Publication Data
Main entry under title:

Reference services in archives.

   (Reference librarian series ; no. 13)
   Includes bibliographies.
   1. Archives—Reference services. I. Whalen, Lucille. II. Series.
CD971.R37 1986   025.5   85-17534
ISBN 0-86656-521-3
ISBN 0-86656-522-1 (pbk.)

Reference Services in Archives

The Reference Librarian
Number 13

CONTENTS

The Reference Process in Archives: An Introduction   1
    Lucille Whalen

Reference Ethics   6
Automated Systems and the Reference Process   7

Remembering the Women: Manuscript Reference at the Schlesinger Library   11
    Katherine Gray Kraft
    Anne Engelhart

Collection Strengths   12
Areas of Research   13
The Library's Users   14
Finding Aids   15
Manuscript Collection Inventories   17
Restricted Collections   20
Effect of Automation   21

Wearing Someone Else's Shoes: Reference in an Established Archive   23
    Edward C. Oetting

Itinerant Archivist   24
Evaluation Process   26
Meeting Research Abilities   28
Reference Policies   29
Legal Concepts   30
Institutional Records   32
Summary   34

The Past in the Present: Reference in a British University Archival Collection   37
   F. W. Ratcliffe

Archival Reference at a Technical University   53
   Elizabeth C. Stewart

  Background   53
  Organization and Arrangement of Collections   54
  Research Use   55
  The Reference Process   56
  Automation   59
  Evaluating Our Reference Service   60
  Conclusion   60

Of Books, Manuscripts and Jars of Snakes: Reference Service in the Museum, Archives and Records Management Section, Toronto Board of Education   63
   Susan McGrath

  Background   64

Life in the Fast Lane: Reference in a Business Archives   81
   Cynthia G. Swank

  Archival Collection   81
  Outside Researchers   83
  Policies and Procedures   83
  Copyright and Access   84
  Processing the Records   85
  Evaluation   86

Researching the Past: An Archivist's Perspective   89
   Frank A. Zabrosky

  Introduction   89
  Archives of Industrial Society   90
  The Reference Inquiry   95

The Paper Chase: Reference Service in the Bank's Archives 105
Anne Van Camp

Historical Background	105
Organization of the Archives	106
Arrangement and Description	107
Automated Information System	108
Reference and Outreach Services	109
Access Policies	110
Evaluation of Reference Services	111

The Challenge of Contemporary Records: Reference Service in a Labor and Urban Archives 113
Philip P. Mason

History From the Bottom Up	113
Archives of Labor and Urban Affairs	114
Factors Affecting Reference	117
Access With Reasonable Restrictions	119
Screening Users	120
Theft and Mutilation: A Continuing Problem	121
Guides to the Collections	123
Audio-Visual Materials	124
Younger Scholars—How Well Prepared?	125
Reference Service: Significant Changes	126

The Manuscript Repository That Isn't 129
Charles Clement

Introduction	129
Reference Service	130
Access	131
Automation and Reference	132
Summary	134

A Well-Kept Secret: The Religious Archive as Reference Resource   137
   Rosalie McQuaide

Historical Background	138
Religious Archival Training and Survey	139
Sisters of Peace	140
Interest in Roots	141
Congregational Archives	144
The Feminist Perspective	145

Reference Service in Catholic Diocesan Archives   149
   James M. O'Toole

Impetus for Renewed Interest	150
Types of Records	151
Role of the Reference Interview	153
Typical Users	154
Trend Toward People History	155
Documenting the Intangible	157

Establishing an Image: The Role of Reference Service in a New Archival Program   159
   Thomas Wilsted

Impetus for a New Archival Program	159
Setting Reference Policies	160
Development of Finding Aids	162
Encouraging the Use of Reference Service	164
Archival Outreach and Reference Services	166
Providing Reference Service	168
Evaluating Reference Services	169
Plans for the Future	171

"What Do You Have on Arthur Flegenheimer?" Research and Reference at the Franklin D. Roosevelt Library   173
   Raymond Teichman

The Roosevelt Legacy	173
Private Donors	175
Processing Collections for Research	175
The Library's Users	177

Preparation for Using the Collection	178
Not Only Manuscripts	179
Publications and Public Education Programs	181
A Mature Library	183

Reference and Research in Regional History Centers   **185**
Glen A. Gildemeister

Regional History Centers: An Introduction	185
Regional Centers and the New Social History	186
Accessing the Center Holdings	187
The Reference Process	190

Expanded Access to Archival Sources   **195**
Thomas Hickerson

A National Register of Historical Manuscripts	196
National Information Systems	199
RLIN Archives and Manuscript Control (AMC)	201
RLIN Implementation and National Development	205

Forthcoming in The Reference Librarian   **209**

The Reference Process in Archives: An Introduction

Lucille Whalen

When the *American Archivist* began publication in 1938, it stated that its primary function was "to serve as the medium through which the common interests and objectives of the profession can be expressed, reiterated, and clearly called to the attention of every group."[1] It is somewhat surprising then that so few articles have been devoted to the reference process in archives. The term *reference*, in fact, is not found in the titles of any articles published in the first twelve volumes, which cover the years 1938 to 1950, and even then the article related to only one aspect of reference—"Some Reference Problems of Picture Collections."[2] This is not to imply that reference service and reference problems were not alluded to in other articles but only that reference as a process in itself seemed less important than many other archival topics, such as preservation, "classification" of manuscripts, analysis of types of records, and education of archivists.

This lack of attention to reference has been pointed out by many in the literature. In one of the early issues of the *American Archivist*, for example, Newsome stated that many archivists see themselves as technicians who are experts in the preservation of records, but "render reference service only as time permits."[3] Again in 1962 the Chairman of the State and Local Records Committee of the Society of American Archivists (SAA) wrote, "It has been several years since we have given much attention to the ultimate use of these records we so carefully preserve because of our preoccupation with the tremendous job of just keeping up with the volume of modern records."[4]

Although other examples of some concern over the lack of attention paid to the reference process in archival literature can be found,

---

The author is Associate Dean and Professor in the School of Library and Information Science, State University of New York at Albany, Albany, New York 12222.

© 1986 by The Haworth Press, Inc. All rights reserved.

the most thorough treatment is given in Saffady's article on "Reference Service to Researchers in Archives."[5] While it is concerned primarily with researchers, much the same could be said for other types of users also. In an effort to determine the extent to which reference had been covered in the literature, Saffady examined the reference section of Evans' *Bibliographic Guide*,[6] a standard work in the field. In summarizing this section, he noted that of the 280 articles in the section, 67 dealt with literary property; 54 with access and confidentiality; 36, estrays, thefts, and replevin; and 30 with examination of suspect documents.

Some of the problems relating to the reference process that Saffady found in the literature included the researcher's lack of orientation to the use of archival materials, the absence of clearly formulated policies concerning the role of the staff in responding to reference requests, and the archivists' lack of knowledge of the collections and the administrative history of the institutions in which they work. Although he concluded that, " . . . there is no historical survey of the development of reference service to researchers in archives that enables us to understand and analyze the ways in which archivists have handled the reference function in the face of pressing administrative duties," in looking to the future, he notes that the application of automated techniques should bring some improvements, particularly in access to collections. However, as archivists today well know, he also pointed out that automation would present new problems, some of which would have a marked effect on the reference process.

Some ten years have passed since this summary, so it seems appropriate to ask whether the reference process has been treated in the literature to any greater extent than previously and whether the problem areas are still the same or have perhaps new ones surfaced.

There may be some significance in the fact that the reference sections in both the Evans *bibliography*—a second edition came out the year after the publication of the Saffady article—and the bibliographies found in the *American Archivist*—comes after chapters on history, administration, appraisal, disposition, preservation, arrangement and description. Considering that sections on access and confidentiality, privacy, copyright, forgeries, estrays and replevin—all related to the reference process but not so closely as the reference interview and the needs of users—it is no wonder that the reference section seems voluminous. As a matter of fact, however, it is far from it. A widely-publicized and excellent work published in

1983, *Archival Theory and Practice in the United States; a Historical Analysis*,[8] has no section on reference, nor is the term even mentioned in the index. Still, there are indications that this trend is changing.

In perusing the increasingly expanding publication list of the SAA, one finds that one of the earlier volumes of the Basic Manual Series is Holbert's *Archives and Manuscripts: Reference and Access*.[9] Admittedly a manual, with more emphasis on the pragmatic than the theoretical, it does, nevertheless, serve to show that reference is a major aspect of an archivist's work, putting it on a par with appraisal, accessioning, arrangement and description of records. In many of the other SAA publications also, e.g., on business, college and university archives, and religious archives, the reference process is included.

In 1984 The National Archives and Records Service published *A Modern Archival Reader: Basic Readings in Archival Theory and Practice*." Although the articles in it are reprinted from other sources, the fact that there is a section devoted to reference again raises the importance of this function in the eyes of the readers. George Chalon, the author of one of the articles, titled simply "Reference," points out the importance of the constant interaction with the user.[10] Because this is what he terms an "action" function and always on-going, there is never time to reflect on the nature of reference itself and to evaluate the process. Chalon points out that the reference process is made up of three elements—records, staff and users.

The records and the way they are organized are a reflection of the way they were created and prepared for use, he goes on to say, and these functions must necessarily take precedence over the needs of the users. Unlike the reference librarian who usually has had no part in the preparation of the materials, the reference archivist—a term used rather infrequently in the literature—has quite often been involved in at least one of the stages of processing the materials and should, therefore, be more familiar with the records. This, of course, is a prime requisite for providing effective reference service.

Regarding the role of the staff in the reference process, he emphasizes the significance of a positive attitude in dealing with researchers and others who use the archives. While there has been a fair amount of writing on the reference interview, relatively little is found in archival literature on the attitudes of archivists in the interview process or in any relationship with users. In the past, archivists, like librarians, did not attempt to hide their attitudes toward genealogists, for example. In fact, they probably concurred, at least in thought, with the archivist who, sympathizing with an official, is said to have uttered "All genealogists should be hanged."[11] Fortunately, the trend toward a more open use of archives and the encouragement of many educators to become more interested in one's roots, genealogists are not only tolerated today, but generally given the same consideration as other users in both libraries and archives.

In discussing users as one of the elements of reference, Chalon notes that while institutions have some degree of control over the quality of the records and the staff, they have little control over the quality of their users. The more prepared the users are, i.e., the more carefully they have studied the secondary sources and planned their research, the more able the archivist is to offer effective assistance. This preparation cannot be taken for granted, however. The literature has been fairly consistent in bemoaning the fact that not only undergraduate students but graduate students and even professional historians often seem to have little or no training in the proper use of archival materials.[12]

The second article in the volume, reprinted from a 1982 issue of the *American Archivist*,[13] from a different viewpoint, i.e., its relationship to arrangement and description and how these affect the user. The author, Mary Jo Pugh, correctly points out that while libraries and archives both have problems in providing effective reference service, they are as different as the kinds of materials they handle, the principles on which their collections are organized, and the methods used in describing materials. Archivists are very much aware of the fact (which librarians tend to forget) that they deal in unique materials and cannot rely on interlibrary loan, cooperative networks and such to retrieve materials needed by the user. Likewise the method of organizing materials through a classification system which makes retrieval easier for librarians is not generally followed by archivists. Again, the description of materials according to provenance, reflecting the processes that created them, rather than describing them primarily for the users, is another difference.

Pugh maintains that it is important to have subject access to collections in addition to a descriptive inventory or register. Some of the assumptions held by archivists, she notes, need to be tested. For example, the archivist subject specialist who is thought to be indispensable may not be the answer to better reference service;

neither should the quality of reference be dependent upon information supplied by the user that is over and above that found in the finding aids. The reference process, she contends, too often depends on the "subject knowledge and memory of the individual archivist and is too dependent on the personalities of the researcher and the archivist."

She goes on to state that not only are there myths and assumptions about the archivist, there are also untested assumptions about users. The concept of the scholar-researcher as the primary user is frequently not substantiated by statistics; the user today is quite often a non-traditional type—administrator, ecologist, urban planner or journalist, and their interests lie in cross-disciplinary research. It is less likely that the archivist will be able to be knowledgeable in such broad-ranging inquiries. Pugh makes a case not only for well-written inventories but also for subject analysis and indexing—time-consuming though they may be for the already overworked archivist. Automated systems may help, she believes, but only if assumptions are clearly identified and needs are precisely and imaginatively spelled out.

Some of the literature has shown archivists' concern for the problems involved in providing reference service, but what do the users have to say? In a 1980 article commenting on the Holbert manual, Carl Brauer, a noted historian, states that he has " . . . infrequently encountered reference archivists who consistently met SAA's high standards."[14] He rather facetiously comments that in his opinion the larger the budget an archives has, the less efficient its reference services are. While most archivists would vehemently disagree with this, he makes a case for a much more rewarding experience working in a small, understaffed archives than in a large, well-funded repository with a large staff and attractive facilities. From the user's viewpoint, he observes, some of the regulations laid down by the archives make little sense, as in the case where he was allowed only one manuscript box at a time and yet, because of the nature of his research, he could examine a box rather quickly and then simply had to wait until another box was brought to him.

Archivists have frequently criticized researchers for not being adequately prepared for the visit. In this same article, however, the author complains about the archivist's somewhat cavalier attitude toward that very preparation. In one instance, for example, Brauer wrote ahead to an archives at some distance about a collection he wanted to use and gave the date when he would arrive. The archivist sent information about the collection but neglected to inform him that the archives would be closed on the date of his proposed visit. Another point of his criticism related to the exit interview, which he said he rarely had in his many visits to archival institutions. He recommended that they should not only become standard procedure but should be accompanied by evaluations of reference services which might later become factors in the assignment of personnel and even in promotions and pay raises for archivists.

In a more recent article, "The User Talks Back,"[15] the author mentioned the lack of preparation on the part of archivists also. Though always being given a courteous, and sometimes enthusiastic, reply when calling ahead to inquire about whether certain materials could be ready when she came on a later date, only once did she actually find that the materials were ready. On these occasions she was usually told that the staff simply did not have time to get the materials ready. Some of the criticisms made by this researcher were rather strongly denied by archivists as being unjustifiably critical and displaying an ignorance regarding the archival profession. One commented on the subject of the archivist being unprepared for the researcher that in his experience, "What often occurs is that researchers fail to show or turn up a day or two late—this after the archivist has gone to considerable trouble in finding the desired items."[16] The examples mentioned may not be typical, but it is likely that there is enough truth in them to make archivists look a bit more closely at their reference procedures.

REFERENCE ETHICS

Some of the problems related in the criticisms of users are touched on in the Code of Ethics for Archivists.[17] A revision of The Archivist's Code, published in 1955, the 1980 Code is accompanied by a longer Commentary which attempts to explain the reasons for some of the statements in the Code itself and to provide a basis for discussion. Those sections most directly related to the reference process are Sections VII, Use and Restrictions, and VIII, Information about Researchers and Correction of Errors. The first directs archivists to answer all reasonable inquiries courteously and with a spirit of helpfulness. It encourages the greatest use of collections compatible with institutional policies, legal considerations, individual rights, and donor agreements. Basic to this encouragement of maximum use is equality of access. All rules regarding the use of the collections should be applied uniformly to all users.

The second section, Information about Researchers . . . , generated considerable discussion among the members of the Code of Ethics Task Force. It states that archivists should not only make materials available for research but should inform researchers that other people are working in the same area since such information can help to avoid duplication and perhaps lead to some type of cooperation among researchers. It is important, however, that archivists do not reveal all the details of another's work. So too must they be sure that a researcher is not prevented from using the same materials another researcher used.

Some of the stipulations of the Code may seem to be a bit of an "overkill" but, as Nancy Lankford[18] reminds us in an article on "Ethics and the Reference Archivist," this probably goes back to the Lowenhein case in which a university historian accused the Roosevelt Library staff of deliberately withholding information regarding the existence of some letters he felt were necessary for his research. He maintained that the staff did this in order to use them exclusively for a volume that was being edited by a staff member. Lankford notes that the most unfortunate aspect of the Lowenheim case was that it revealed a lack of trust between historians and archivists. Though the incident is probably forgotten by most, there is still the occasional tension between historian and archivist. For the most part, however, the past several years have seen a greater cooperation among all the groups interested in the preservation and use of historical records. Lankford comments that perhaps the tensions were timely, leading as they did to a growing awareness of the archivist's responsibilities and to expanded and new organizations which provided forums to discuss the "nuances of ethical considerations and gave archivists the wherewithal to meet the challenges they faced."[19]

AUTOMATED SYSTEMS AND THE REFERENCE PROCESS

The area that has received so much coverage in the literature—automation—is very much related to the reference process as it directly affects the way archivists work with their users. The profession has come a long way from the early days of the SPINDEX system which at one time was thought to be the answer to the access problems so many archivists were groping for. The National Information Systems Task Force (NISTF), appointed by SAA in 1977, though long after many individual institutions attempted to implement their own systems, admits that it had some difficulty in knowing precisely what it was to do and how it was to go about it. Lytle tells his readers " . . . to discard any notion that NISTF progressed in an orderly fashion from the project's inception to its completion."[20] Nevertheless, as Lytle goes on to describe, NISTF was able to dispel the idea of *a* national information system and concentrate on such aspects as developing a comprehensive data element dictionary, establishing a new MARC format based on AACR-2, which was accepted by SAA and ALA, study the information environment for archives, and continue to maintain communication with the archival community.

The entire issue of the *American Archivist* for fall 1984 was devoted to the automation of archives—its history, appraisal, planning, and application of new technologies. It shows how far the profession has come even since a similar issue was published in 1979. The implications for reference are many, as the library profession has most certainly seen. Perhaps it would be well to return to the final statement Saffady made in his article regarding the effects of automation on the reference process, " . . . the day may be coming, if it is not already here, when researchers in archives will not make time for reference service. [That is, researchers can sit in front of their terminals and printers at home or in their offices and get the materials they need.] When that happens, an important dimension will be lost in both archival work and historical research."[21] A more concerted effort on the part of archivists not only to use the new technology to its best advantage in the reference process but to present a better understanding of what effective reference is to researchers and other users on all levels, should, it is hoped, preclude the situation Saffady describes.

It is intended that the present volume will be a step toward a more comprehensive treatment of the reference process in archives. It is not intended to cover all aspects of the problem, nor to describe reference in all types of archives. Rather, it attempts to give a picture of the reference process as it is found in some types of archival environments for the librarian who may or may not be familiar with archives and for those archivists, especially those new to the field, who wish to know more about the reference process in different types of institutions. It will be evident that archives is frequently used to mean both records and manuscript collections. It should be evident also that the archives and manuscript collections described have both similarities and differences in the way in which reference is practiced, but these contribute to making both the reference archivist's and the user's tasks more enjoyable—at least in so far as one thrives on new discoveries and challenges.

ENDNOTES

1. Karl Trever. "The *American Archivist*: The Voice of a Profession," *American Archivist* 15:1 (January 1952), 147.
2. Hermine M. Baumhofer. "Some Reference Problems of Picture Collections," *American Archivist* 13:2 (April 1950), 121-128.
3. Albert Ray Newsome. "The Archivist in American Scholarship," *American Archivist* 2:4 (October 1939), 217.
4. William T. Alderson in a letter to Frank B. Evans, September 5, 1962. Quoted in Frank B. Evans. "The State Archivist and the Researcher." *American Archivist* 26:3 (July 1963), 321.
5. William Saffady. "Reference Service to Researchers in Archives," *RQ* 14 (Winter 1974), 139-144.
6. Frank B. Evans. *The Administration of Modern Archives; A Select Bibliographic Guide* (Washington, D.C.: National Archives and Records Service, 1970), 72-82.
7. Saffady, p. 139.
8. Richard C. Berner. *Archival Theory and Practice in the United States: A Historical Analysis.* (Seattle: University of Washington, 1983).
9. Sue E. Holbert. *Archives and Manuscripts: Reference and Access.* (Chicago: Society of American Archivists, 1977).
10. *Modern Archival Reader: Basic Readings in Archival Theory and Practice.* (Washington, D.C.: National Archives and Records Service, 1984).
11. McCain, W.D. "The Public Relations of Archival Depositories," *American Archivist* 3:4 (October 1940), 235.
12. See Saffady, pp. 140-41. He cites several authors on the lack of proper preparation of researchers, e.g., Walter Rundel and Philip C. Brooks.
13. Mary Jo Pugh. "The Illusion of Omniscience: Subject Access and the Reference Archivist," *American Archivist* 45:1 (Winter 1982): 33-44.
14. Carl M. Brauer. "Researcher Evaluation of Reference Services," *American Archivist* 43:1 (Winter 1980): 77.
15. Mary N. Speakman. "The User Talks Back," American Archivist 47:2 (Spring 1984): 164-171.
16. In Letters to the Editor. American Archivist 43:4 (Fall 1984): 353.
17. *American Archivist* 43:4 (Fall 1980): 414-415; Commentary follows on pp. 415-418.
18. Nancy Lankford. "Ethics and the Reference Archivist," *The Midwestern Archivist* 8:1 (1983): 7-13.
19. Lankford, p. 13.
20. Richard Lytle. "An Analysis of the Work of the National Information Systems Task Force," *American Archivist* 47:4 (Fall 1984): 358.
21. Saffady, p. 143.

Remembering the Women: Manuscript Reference at the Schlesinger Library

Katherine Gray Kraft
Anne Engelhart

The Arthur and Elizabeth Schlesinger Library on the History of Women in America is a noncirculating research library open to the public. A department of Radcliffe College, the library was founded as the Women's Archives in 1943 with the donation of alumna Maud Wood Park's extensive collection of manuscript and published materials on the campaign for woman suffrage in the United States.[1] The Woman's Rights Collection, as Park's gift was named, was soon augmented by documents from historian Mary Beard on her unsuccessful attempt to establish a World Center for Women's Archives. Beard also directed to the Women's Archives the papers of other women and organizations originally promised to the World Center. In 1949, the Women's Archives was opened to the public. Over the next twenty years, the archives acquired collections of individual women, families, and organizations representing a wide variety of occupations, ideas, and issues.

The Women's Archives moved to larger quarters in 1967. It was then renamed to honor the late historian Arthur Schlesinger, Sr. (1888-1965), and his wife, Elizabeth Bancroft Schlesinger (1887-1977). A member of the Harvard History Department and a trustee of Radcliffe, Professor Schlesinger had served as chairman of the Advisory Committee of the Women's Archives (1950-1963), and was instrumental in the growth and development of the archives. Elizabeth Bancroft Schlesinger maintained an interest in the library for the remainder of her life; she had published articles on American women long before such topics were popular.

Ms. Kraft, on leave for 1984-1985, is Associate Curator of Manuscripts at the Arthur and Elizabeth Schlesinger Library on the History of Women in America at Radcliffe College, Cambridge, MA 02138. Ms. Engelhart is taking her place for the year as Assistant Curator.

© 1986 by The Haworth Press, Inc. All rights reserved.

The "second women's movement," with its beginnings in the 1960s, was influencing all of society by the early 1970s; academic circles were not immune. Attempts to recover women's past were carried out by activists seeking to understand the roots of contemporary woman's condition and to find examples of courageous women to emulate, as well as by scholars concerned with restoring women to their place in history. The library's books, periodicals, vertical files, photographs, and manuscript collections proved an ideal resource.

COLLECTION STRENGTHS

Today, the Schlesinger Library's holdings fill approximately 5500 linear feet and consist of nearly 700 large collections and more than 900 small collections (these numbers include both processed and unprocessed papers). The library continues to build on its traditional strengths, adding new areas that complement and enlarge upon the older collections. For manuscript holdings, these strengths lie mainly in the areas of women's rights, suffrage, feminism, and the contemporary women's movement; women in government, politics, and the legal professions; employment and trade union activities; education; religion and missions; medicine, health and reproductive issues; social welfare and reform; the family and domesticity; women's organizations and organizations devoted to women's issues; prominent, unusual and enterprising women; and the history of women's history and women's studies. Examples of women represented by individual or family collections include Susan B. Anthony, Elizabeth Blackwell, Betty Friedan, Emma Goldman, Alice and Edith Hamilton, Elizabeth Holtzman, Jeannette Rankin, Adrienne Rich, Lucy Stone, and Harriet Beecher Stowe. The library is just as concerned with collecting illuminating papers of nonnotable women, and has numerous such collections; a list of their names would not, however, reveal very much. Organizational archives include the records of the Lydia E. Pinkham Medicine Company, National Organization for Women, North Bennet Street Industrial School, and the Women's Educational and Industrial Union of Boston.

The library does not ordinarily solicit papers of women involved primarily in literary, artistic, or scientific fields, as they are more likely to be appropriately represented in repositories specializing in those subjects. The library's holdings do include the papers of a number of scientists, artists, and writers; these papers are here, however, because the particular women were pioneers in their fields or because they were actively concerned with women's place in their professions or in society.[2] Once almost alone in acquiring documentation of women's lives, the library now competes and cooperates with numerous institutions that have come to realize that "women's history" is an important aspect of all history.

AREAS OF RESEARCH

Because women were neglected as the objects of historical and social scientific study until recently, the number of unexplored questions is almost limitless. In addition to biographies and histories of organizations, movements, professions, and social policies, researchers at the Schlesinger Library are investigating women's attitudes toward marriage, childbirth, death, divorce, women's rights, and careers; the nature of relationships between women and between women and men; the effect of technological development on the lives of average women; the role of religion in women's lives; the dynamics of family decision-making; courtship patterns; the role of women in political parties; relationships between women of different classes; and so forth.

Researchers learn of the library's existence through word of mouth, footnotes in books and other publications, and through a variety of reference works. The most complete listing of the holdings is contained in *Arthur and Elizabeth Schlesinger Library on the History of Women in America: The Manuscript Inventories and the Catalogs of Manuscripts, Books, and Periodicals* (Boston: G.K. Hall, 1984), a ten-volume set consisting of all the public finding aids available in the library in the fall of 1983 (when they were photographed). Another invaluable resource for women's studies researchers, *Women's History Sources* (New York: Bowker, 1979), contains brief descriptions of individual collections in nearly 1600 U.S. repositories, as well as an extensive subject index; the Schlesinger Library is represented by more than 650 entries. In addition, the library reports to the *National Union Catalog of Manuscript Collections, American Literary Manuscripts,* the *Directory of Archives and Manuscript Repositories in the U.S.,* Lee Ash's *Subject Collections,* and various subject area reference guides and historical editing projects. On a smaller scale, general descriptions of the library and its holdings are included in the *Directory of Archives and Manuscript Repositories at Harvard University and Radcliffe College*, and *Photographs at Harvard and Radcliffe: A Directory*. The library publishes both a biennial report and, in alternate years, a newsletter; both describe new acquisitions and projects.

In 1949, the year the Women's Archives opened, seven researchers appeared. In 1969-1970, there were 247. By 1976, 3,200 research visits were recorded and more than 5,270 in 1983-1984; in that year the library also received nearly 1,000 mail and telephone inquiries. An average of 50 researchers, many of whom are first-time users, visit the manuscript division each month.

THE LIBRARY'S USERS

As part of an effort to understand more precisely who uses the library, the staff compiles a monthly statistical summary. All unpublished holdings (whether manuscripts, tapes, oral histories, or photos) must be requested in writing. Completed manuscript request forms are sorted by number of individual researchers, as well as by total number of research requests (ultimately the forms are arranged by manuscript collection). The number of requests coming in by mail and by phone and the number of questions concerning photographs exclusively are also counted each month. Staff members keep a running tally of questions asked in person. In November 1984, for example, 133 manuscript request forms were filed by 67 different researchers. There were 52 in-person manuscript reference questions and 16 questions concerning photos; 22 research requests were answered by mail, and 38 by telephone.

There is no manuscript reference staff as such. The curator and associate curator (who work full time) and three part-time staff members devote whatever time is needed to in-person and telephone reference; the assistant to the director handles mail inquiries. Beyond accounting for sheer numbers, the staff asks researchers who are Harvard/Radcliffe undergraduates to identify themselves as such (in 1983-1984 they accounted for thirteen percent of total use), and seeks, informally, to learn of readers' research interests.

Though the library contains major resources for researchers seeking to understand many different aspects of American history, the manuscript collections are used primarily by academic researchers interested in women's history or in the wider field of women's studies, which encompasses the social sciences and the humanities. The growing interest in women's past, however and the library's efforts at "outreach" (which include a slide show on women's history for use by high schools, clubs, or others unfamiliar with the field, exhibits, and a variety of public events such as workshops, lectures, and colloquia), continue to bring a wider variety of users to the Schlesinger Library than to many other research libraries. Schoolchildren, undergraduates, community organizers, journalists, and other nonacademics are among those who take advantage of the library's open access policy.

The researcher using original documents in several repositories is likely to be confronted with a bewildering array of admission requirements, rules, and reference tools. Each repository has its own area of specialization, its own regulations, and its own system of finding aids. In some cases, there are no written sources of information about the holdings and the researcher is totally dependent on the curator's presence, knowledge, memory, and good will. In others, every document is listed separately in the card catalog and/or in calendars, registers, or inventories; such item processing usually provides no subject access nor any overall description of collections. In still other repositories, collection finding aids list containers or series only; the researcher might learn that there are thirty cartons of correspondence without being told any further details.

The reader unfamiliar with manuscript research is often discouraged by its diffuse nature. A book is written to communicate specific information, but a manuscript collection encompasses papers written not as historical documents but for various personal, practical, legal, economic, or other purposes. Research in manuscript collections is much more time-consuming than most people expect; in most cases the finding aid cannot possibly point out every person, group, event, or subject represented in a collection. It is helpful to understand how finding aids are constructed in order to know how best to use them efficiently.

FINDING AIDS

Although many manuscript collections include publications or photocopies, the preponderance of papers within each collection is unpublished and unique. How these physically discrete and often disparate papers are arranged depends on a variety of factors, among them whether there was a logical order at the time of donation; the proportion of identified correspondents and dated letters (to suggest whether to impose an alphabetical or chronological arrangement); the variety and bulk of different types of papers (e.g., diaries, financial records, etc.); and the presence of restricted material. At the Schlesinger Library the processor discusses possible arrangements as well as the appropriate level of description for each collection with the curator.

Any collection can be arranged in only one way, but access to its various parts must be provided in a multiplicity of ways by means of the description. The description—which at the Schlesinger Library consists of an inventory and catalog cards—must reveal the connections among the papers and also, as much as reasonably possible, their content; the latter need is met partly by providing numerous access points through the card catalog and in some cases through an index to all or part of the inventory. The two-part finding aid system in use at the library—with the inventories serving as tables of contents to collections and the card catalog as a common index to all the inventories—seems to work well both for researchers pursuing questions on their own and for staff helping readers or doing their own research. At the same time it provides a way to establish an appropriate degree of intellectual control sufficiently speedy (though still time-consuming) that the staff have been able to provide some control over virtually all the collections in the library.[3] In its basic structure this system conforms to the best current thinking in the archival profession. It conforms also in the philosophy that it reflects: that it is practically and ethically necessary to put down on paper (or eventually on some magnetic medium) as much of one's knowledge of a collection as is reasonably possible. No processor or curator lives, or stays at the same job, forever. At the same time, this need must be balanced with the need to process as many collections as possible; completeness and perfection are always out of reach.

The manuscript collections in the Schlesinger Library range in size and complexity from a single letter, with known author, recipient, date, and topic, to hundreds of cartons containing correspondence, memoranda, reports, speeches, photographs, diaries, scrapbooks, and so forth, with portions unidentified, undated, or fragmented. Each collection has an inventory describing its contents; the usual level at which papers are described is the file unit, which is a folder, volume, or any other object (e.g., a plaque) that can stand on its own in a document box. The library's manuscript card catalog serves as an index to the inventories for "large" collections (those that can stand alone on a shelf), and as an index directly to "small" collections (those that are smaller than a half document box), oral histories, dissertations, and tapes. Together, the catalog and inventories are the basic tools for all manuscript reference in the library.

All researchers coming to the Schlesinger Library first register at the reception desk and store their personal belongings in lockers. Those needing unpublished holdings are directed to the manuscript reading room. Due to the lack of a separate reference staff, there is no routine reference interview at the beginning or end of a reader's period of research. Copies of instructions for the use of the finding aids are prominently displayed, along with a sign urging those with further questions to "inquire within." Readers tend to consult the staff as questions arise, and the staff relies on passing conversations with these users to keep informed of their successes and difficulties. Observant researchers often point out discrepancies or omissions in the card catalog and in inventories. Further subject headings, for example, are often added when a user can show that a particular collection has not been adequately cataloged.

The small size of the staff, which precludes a formal, systematic approach to reference, has one unintended advantage: if all staff members process manuscript collections and all do reference work, then processors automatically understand reference needs and produce better finding aids.

MANUSCRIPT COLLECTION INVENTORIES

Inventories for the large collection are kept alphabetically in thesis binders on top of the card catalog. Each inventory begins with a heading giving the names and dates of the creator(s) of the collection, inclusive dates of the papers, quantity, information on the donor, dates of receipt and processing, restrictions on access and use, and accession numbers. Next is a biography or organizational or family history. When the creator(s) is/are well known, biographical notes are brief, citing available published sources. Scope and content notes follow, giving a general description of the collection (by series, if any), pointing out sections or items of particular interest, types of material not included (e.g., some collections document only a professional life and include no personal correspondence), and location of additional papers, if known. The introductory material concludes with a list of additional catalog entries and is followed by a series list and the inventory proper, which lists the contents of file units. Currently individual items are noted only in exceptional cases, although in older inventories this practice is more common. The scope and content note indicates in general the subject matter of the papers. For each collection the existence of photographs, audio-and video-tapes, or other nonmanuscript materials—stored separately for preservation reasons—is noted in the inventory, usually with the relevant manuscript material, but sometimes (in older inventories) at the end.

A correspondents' index concludes the inventory. It usually includes writers and recipients (distinguished by different symbols). Nearly all such indexes are selective, as most collections include single or a few letters from or to obscure persons. This is especially true of large, contemporary collections; few researchers need easy access to the letters of a particular "unknown" individual. A complete index to the mail received by the National Organization for Women would be of little use to anyone, but a selective index of well-known leaders of the women's movement such as Betty Friedan and Gloria Steinem would be useful to many researchers.

Added catalog entries for individuals, organizations, and subjects are chosen after the collection is sorted, arranged, and inventoried. Subject cataloging cannot be exhaustive, and is thus necessarily idiosyncratic. To minimize such idiosyncrasy, this task is carried out in consultation with the curator. It requires a general familiarity with the specific collection; a wide-ranging knowledge of people, organizations, and events prominent in traditional as well as women's history; and an acquaintance with the library's related holdings, current and future research interests, and Library of Congress subject headings. Separate cumulative cards distinguish those collections containing papers by specific individuals or organizations from those containing papers about them. Subject headings, assigned to each collection as a whole and not to individual items within a collection, include the donor's occupation, ethnicity, and geographic region, as well as dominant themes found in the papers (e.g., "Courtship" for a series of love letters, or "Health" for letters recounting various illnesses in the family). The staff has adapted LC subject headings both to simplify the card catalog and to reflect the holdings more accurately. Since all the collections in the Library relate to women, headings prefixed by "Women as" or "Women—" are redundant, and would slow filing and reference; in most cases, subjects are listed without "women" as a modifier (e.g., "Authors," or "Education"). The phrase "Women in . . ." has been retained, however, for use with countries and with broad occupational categories. For example, papers of a missionary doctor describing her travels through India and work with female patients would include headings for "Physicians," "Missionaries," "Women in India," and "India—Description and travel." Some headings used for a number of years by the library have more recently been adopted by the Library of Congress, such as "Feminism," and "Sex discrimination." Others, such as "Dual careers," while not unique to the library, are not (yet) officially sanctioned.

Following preparation of the inventory, the processor writes a one-card description of the collection to serve as the main entry card in the catalog. The name of the individual or organization that created the collection serves as the main entry and functions analogously to that of the author of a book. The front of the main entry card contains the call number; main entry with birth and death dates, or dates of founding and dissolution; inclusive dates of the papers; and size of the collection. A brief paragraph identifies the creator(s) and describes the types of papers. Restrictions, if any, are also indicated but not in detail. The back of the card carries tracings or information on where they may be found.

Unlike added entries for proper names (individual or corporate), which appear on cumulative cards (see above), subject added entries appear on copies of the main entry card, as in book cataloging. Presumably, a researcher interested in a specific person or group would need to see all papers by or about that entity, and so would want to read all the relevant inventories to locate and request appropriate documents: a full main entry card would in most cases be of little use. By contrast, a researcher interested in diaries by New England schoolteachers in the 1880s, for instance, can choose or eliminate collections by use of the full entry cards. Such subject added entries, while useful for almost any kind of research, are essential for work in a field such as women's history, where the emphasis lies less on notables than on the lives and experiences of the "average" person.

The staff attempts to produce some kind of finding aid for every manuscript collection in the library. In the late 1970s preliminary processing was introduced to make the large backlog of unprocessed collections—some acquired ten or more years earlier—available for research. Preliminary processing may consist merely of reboxing existing folders in standard, acid-free records center cartons and writing a folder list with the briefest possible introductory material and the most rudimentary cataloging. More often new folders are needed and there is at least some attempt at a logical arrangement, a biography, a scope and content note, and more extensive, though still preliminary, cataloging. A few collections that are very large or to which access is restricted, or both, have only very general descriptions; otherwise the difference between preliminary and final descriptions is one of degree rather than kind.

The so-called small collections are processed in the same way as large collections, but their inventories are filed only with the papers and not in the manuscript reading room. Researchers must rely on the main entry card to tell them enough about the creator and contents of any one of these small collections so that they can decide whether they need to see it.

RESTRICTED COLLECTIONS

Most of the collections in the library are unrestricted and open to research. Some are wholly or partially restricted because of the sensitive nature of the documents they contain. In some cases, restrictions are requested by the donor; in others, the library, in consultation with the donor, has imposed restrictions. By placing or allowing restrictions, the staff hopes both to encourage donors to save, rather than destroy, controversial documents, and to protect the confidentiality of donors or others who are authors or subjects of papers in a collection. The inventory specifies the restrictions on a particular collection and the staff will give the researcher additional information when necessary.[4]

In addition to collections of manuscripts, the manuscript division processes oral histories (transcripts and tapes), photographs, paper copies of dissertations, and audio- and video-cassettes. With the exception that many more additional catalog entries are assigned to each item, the cataloging of oral histories, dissertations, and cassettes is similar to that for published materials.

The library's photographs, numbering more than 20,000 in processed manuscript and photograph collections, and as many again in unprocessed collections, receive increasingly heavy use. To protect the photos from frequent handling and exposure to light, those in processed collections have been microfilmed. The library receives at least as many inquiries for photos to illustrate particular themes or periods as for portraits of particular women. Subject cataloging for photographs is therefore essential. Subject headings are based on those in *Subject Headings Used in the Library of Congress, Prints and Photographs Division* (preliminary edition, 1980), and are modified as necessary. Included are headings for chronological period, some photographic processes (e.g., daguerreotype, tintype), photographer (if known), geographic location, and subjects. An extensive inventory of the photographs gives all known information for each photo, including size. Using the catalog, it is now possible to locate identification numbers assigned to photos of suffrage parades, clerical workers, domestic interiors, and so forth, to read a full description of each relevant photo, and to view it on microfilm. A key lists microfilm frame numbers corresponding to the photo identification numbers. Paper prints from the microfilm are provided at the library; staff will order photographic prints from Harvard's Fogg Museum. Although describing and cataloging the thousands of photos is a time-consuming and difficult project, the efficiency and greater thoroughness it has brought to the reference process are immeasurable. Eventually, all cataloging information—subject headings, descriptions, photo identification numbers, and microfilm frame numbers—will be part of an in-house database, readily accessible to staff as a complete unit both on-line and in printed form.

EFFECT OF AUTOMATION

And what of the future? The advent of automation in the form of three microcomputers has already altered many of the daily office functions of the library, particularly through the use of word processing and database management software. Inventories, for example, are now entered and stored on the hard disk of an IBM XT. It is hoped that within the next year the library will have compiled a database of the library's photograph collection. It is inevitable, too, that automation will come to play an important part in how records concerning each manuscript collection (i.e., control files) are maintained. The Schlesinger Library is currently participating in a two-year survey at Harvard and Radcliffe (funded by the National Historical Publications and Records Commission) that seeks to identify and describe every sizable manuscript collection within the university. Information about each collection will be entered through

RLIN, the on-line utility of the Research Libraries Group, and will appear as part of the university's union catalog (which now appears on microfiche and will in time be on-line). For every record, this on-line database will allow each individual library a screen—not accessible to researchers—for its control file. Thus a summary of pertinent information concerning a collection—for instance, its conservation status, location numbers, notes on donor relations and future actions—would appear as a unified record.

Nor will automation provide the only impetus towards change. As of this writing plans are under way for an extensive renovation and expansion of the library's facilities, and, concomitant with these proposals, a reorganization of reference service for the entire library. It is likely that a central reference desk located next to a union catalog, standard reference books, and one or more terminals (among other reference tools), will serve as the first stop for users of manuscript, printed, and audiovisual material. Researchers requiring more information will then be directed to the curators of the respective divisions. Users will thus more formally be introduced to the wealth of material housed at the library and alerted to the intrinsic connections among its manuscripts, books, periodicals, photographs, and other holdings. Ideally, an exit interview will be conducted with each researcher so that both instruction and finding aids may be improved. Increased informed communication between users and reference staff will facilitate the shared goal of more efficient, more thorough research and an improved understanding of our past.

ENDNOTES

1. This synopsis of the library's history is based on the *40th Anniversary Report* (1983) of the Schlesinger Library by Patricia Miller King, Director.
2. A copy of the library's "Collection Development Policies" may be obtained from the library, 10 Garden Street, Cambridge, Massachusetts, 02138.
3. Curator of Manuscripts Eva Mosley is largely responsible for improving and standardizing the finding aids now in use. The authors would also like to acknowledge Ms. Mosley's invaluable assistance in preparing this article.
4. For a discussion of restrictions on the records of contemporary feminist organizations, see Katherine Gray Kraft, "The Public and the Personal: Archives of Women's Activist Organizations," *Radcliffe Quarterly* 70:1 (March 1984): 9-10.

Wearing Someone Else's Shoes: Reference in an Established Archive

Edward C. Oetting

If the thought of wearing someone else's shoes gives one pause, then consider the plight of the archivist accepting a new position at an established archives or manuscript collection. Like our feet, each archival or manuscript repository is unique or very nearly so in its subject area covered, in its collections held, in its clientele and in the way, often idiosyncratic to a fault, in which it describes and makes available its resources.

Indeed, to carry this inelegant and pedestrian analogy further, just as our own feet are not a perfect match, left to right, practices and procedures within a single repository often are not consistent in application even within specific categories of material. Some manuscript or archival collections may be described at the series level, some at the item level; some photographs may receive a brief description and listing in a printed index or inventory; some may be accorded full AACR II, cradle-to-grave cataloging.

The key word in an understanding of this analogy is "unique." It is the uniqueness of the size and shape of our feet that makes the thought of wearing another's shoes painful. It is the uniqueness of our archival collections and missions that reduces consistency of treatment and standards of practice in the archival profession to a few accepted principles and techniques. The whole archival profession is built on a theory (provenance) which lets each collection dictate to the professional how it should be organized, described, and made available. To our librarian colleagues engaged in bringing conformity in practice to the classification and description of individual items, archivists must seem an anarchic lot bent on being the dog assiduously wagged by its tail.

The reference transaction in an academic archives or indeed in any archives or manuscript repository is the place where the other

---

Mr. Oetting is Head, Arizona Collections, and University Archivist at Arizona State University, Tempe, Arizona 85287.

shoe finally drops (the last foot cliche) in terms of the patron and the archivist paying the price for the uniqueness of its collections and the lack of standardization of practice. Because archival collections are both non-browsable and non-circulating, the patron's only intellectual interface with the primary materials he or she seeks is through the reference archivist and the finding aids created for that repository's collection. Experience gained researching archival materials one collection is rarely transferrable to research conducted elsewhere.

ITINERANT ARCHIVIST

My professional experience has reflected to some degree the "itinerant archivist" nature of this profession. I have worked as Assistant Curator of Manuscripts/University Archivist at the University of North Dakota, University Archivist/Campus Records Officer at the State University of New York at Albany; and currently as Head, Arizona Collections and University Archives at Arizona State University. The titles of my positions alone indicate the diversity of job responsibilities that most professional archivists are required to undertake. My current position assumes responsibility for regional manuscript collections, university archives and records management.

All this is stated not to trumpet the importance of my positions but to indicate both the diversity and specificity of knowledge required by those positions. This diversity and specificity are what can easily make reference work in a new position the most daunting and challenging of an individual's responsibilities.

Diversity in types of collections and formats of materials acquired almost pre-supposes idiosyncracy of practice in a profession with little or no standardization. Thus, for example, the way photographs are made available in one repository likely will not be duplicated in another repository. Card files and indexes for manuscript material in one archives will be paper inventories or simple container lists in another.

The intense specificity of each repository's mission and subject area increase the likelihood of "local" approaches to the reference process. As all archival and manuscript repositories are geographical, institutional or subject-oriented in nature, there is obviously great emphasis placed upon comprehensive knowledge of the area, institution or subject in question. A university archivist, for example, is expected to know or be able to find out all there is to know about his or her university. A manuscript curator in an "Arizona Collection" or a "North Dakota Room" is responsible for making very specific information about those areas readily accessible. The intensity of the specificity needed and the "localness" of the information desired make it likely that the vehicles for providing that information will be "homegrown" and non-transferrable outside that repository.

If the reference process demanded that each new archivist possess upon arrival the in-depth knowledge specific to that repository, then the concept of the professional archivist would lose most if not all meaning. It is unlikely to assume, for example, that through prior academic training or experience one individual would possess a strong knowledge of the history and development of the states of Arizona and North Dakota and of the State University of New York at Albany. This is both learned knowledge and knowledge that is learnable.

To return to the reference process, that knowledge necessary is not only learnable but is accessible or should be through the reference tools, catalogs and finding aids provided to the researcher. It is, then, not the responsibility of the professional archivist to possess previous knowledge of each individual area, institution or subject in which he or she might be involved. Instead, it is the professional responsibility of that individual to evaluate and increase the effectiveness of the repository in meeting the informational needs of its patrons. And it is through the reference process and reference tools that those needs are evaluated and met.

The scenario of the itinerant archivist traveling from institution to institution is a valid one—at least from this individual's perspective. Also valid is the degree to which the reference tools mold each archivist's knowledge of the holdings of the repository and the history of the institution, region or subject covered. This is particularly true in the case of a college or university archives. Often the only recorded, preserved or available information concerning that institution is found in the institution's archives. There are few, if any, secondary sources available to rely upon for the history of most institutions. Therefore, if the reference tools available to the newly appointed archivist are idiosyncratic and only supplemental to the knowledge of the former archivist, as is often the case (in most small academic archives, the true and most detailed catalog of the repository holdings lies in the brain of the archivist), then the new archivist faces some very difficult decisions very quickly.

Having worked in academic archives established by my predecessors, I have always, at least initially, had to work with reference tools and systems established by someone else. This can be both disconcerting and dislocating to the new archivist. The newly appointed archivist should begin an immediate ongoing evaluation of the efficacy of the repository's reference tools and reference service. The archivist's evaluation will evolve as he or she becomes more familiar with these tools and services. Quick decisions on implementing new reference systems or services should be avoided except in cases where the incomplete nature or eccentricities of those tools both force and allow a relatively quick change.

EVALUATION PROCESS

The evaluation process for reference tools and services consists of two sets of factors: factors that have a specific relationship to each institution and factors that are more general and based upon accepted principles of professional service. Factors in the first category include such questions as: Are the finding aids understandable? Do they comprehensively cover the collection? Can they be kept up-to-date and current with present and future staffing levels? If the answers to these and similar questions are yes, then in most instances those finding aids and systems should be continued.

If the answers to some or all were no, then there are several other questions that need to be asked. First, the three questions asked of the old systems should be applied as test questions to the formulation of any new reference system. If answered affirmatively, then additional questions arise. For example, can the old system be closed without a major disruption in service? Will the time devoted to creating a new system significantly increase the level of service or ease of maintenance in comparison with the old system? Does the new system solve the problems associated with the old one without creating new ones?

If all the above questions are answered affirmatively and the decision is made to change or seriously revise the archives' reference tools, rules and regulations, then the second phase of the evaluation process begins. There are, in my experience, three major factors that must be addressed in any successful overall reference policy for an academic archives. They are: (1) The constituencies of the repository; (2) rules and policy regarding use and accessibility of archival material; and (3) the reference tools and finding aids for the intellectual control of archival material. Reference tools and practices for any academic archives must be developed on or incorporate these three components.

The constituencies of an academic archives should determine to a great degree the type and level of reference tools and service available. It is in the area of constituencies that one finds the greatest degree of difference between a college or university archives and a manuscript repository or research collection. The explicit primary goal of manuscript collections is to acquire and preserve primary source material in order to make it available for serious research or educational purposes. Therefore, the majority of patrons of a manuscript collection in an academic setting should be individuals engaged in scholarship, study at the undergraduate or graduate level, or personal research. Although the actual constituency of a manuscript collection often includes patrons such as lawyers, journalists, architectural consultants and genealogists who use the materials for commercial or non-educational purposes, nevertheless, the mission of a manuscript repository in a college or university is indeed "academic" and as such pre-supposes that the material will be used primarily for academic purposes.

A college or university archives, on the other hand, has both a broader mission and constituency. Although most such archives are established to acquire, preserve and make available primary source material relating to the history and development of its parent institution, a modern university archives also serves a research function for the college or university administration. It keeps and makes accessible records that have not only historical value but those having administrative, informational or evidential value. Indeed, it could be argued that an academic archives' primary constituency is its administration. Without careful attention to the administration's informational demands, the viability and continued support for that archives is uncertain at best.

This role for the university administration as prime constituent has several implications for an archives' reference service. The most demanding is the "drop everything else" nature of reference requests. There is no real way to plan for this in terms of reference tools or services; it is more an intensification of a research request than a request that is somehow different in nature from other such requests. Another implication is that the reference tools and finding aids must be understandable to the offices whose records they were originally. In requesting materials or information from non-current files, offices rely on memory and knowledge of that offices' filing system. Even if the concept of "sanctity of the original order" did not hold sway, it would not be worthwhile to change the arrangement of accessioned records.

MEETING RESEARCH ABILITIES

The ability level of a repository's constituency to conduct research also needs to be taken into consideration. The level and extent to which indexing and cataloging occur may depend upon the type of constituency using those materials. Experienced researchers are more often able to handle the brief descriptions and folder-level arrangement and description prevalent in most archives than are casual or inexperienced researchers. Therefore an archival repository whose constituency is primarily undergraduates and administrators, for example, might need more detailed finding aids than a repository whose primary constituency is the graduate student or scholar.

The determination of the type and extent of reference services provided, then, depends a great deal on the constituencies an archival repository serves or was established to serve. Decisions concerning both the desired and actual constituencies (not always the same) depend upon the stated mission and goals for the repository and the actual patron mix as indicated by the archives' use statistics.

Every academic archives or manuscript collection should have a mission or policy statement that indicates what, why, and for whom the repository is acquiring, preserving and making available primary source material. Such a policy may be written so broadly as to include the entire state of residence, or in the case of a college or university, may indicate that material is acquired to foster educational or research purposes. Implicitly or explicitly the parameters of a repository could be tightened to focus on the "scholarly" community, i.e., graduate students or faculty. No matter how loosely written or communicated, the new archivist needs to ascertain what specific constituencies the repository exists to serve. Such determination will have direct impact upon the level and type of reference services provided.

Most academic archives have a gap between the designated and actual constituency of that repository. It can be safely stated that most archivists hope to serve the "serious scholar." It is this individual for whom primary source material, the "jewels" or any archives, is acquired. It is also safe to say that for most archival and manuscript collections, the serious scholar quantitatively makes up a small minority of the clientele.

There is only one way to determine an academic archives' actual constituencies and that is systematically and accurately to keep patron and use statistics. Every academic archives should record the number of users by patron groups and the number and types of materials used regardless of the size of the repository. Patrons can be grouped into the following categories: undergraduate, graduate, faculty, administrative staff, and public. These are distinct and easily discernible patron groups, and information gained concerning the percentage of users in each category constitutes significant information for determining appropriate levels of reference service. The measurement of use by type of material or format is the other statistical measure necessary for any evaluation of reference services.

REFERENCE POLICIES

The second component of any reference program in an academic archives concerns the rules and policies governing the use of and access to materials in the repository. The one mission common to all archival repositories is the permanent preservation of its primary source material. By definition, archival quality conveys the implication of permanent retention. And, difficult as it sometimes is to acknowledge emotionally, permanent retention in the archival sense means forever. Therefore, it is essential that archival or manuscript materials' point of greatest interaction with the public, i.e., the reference transaction occur in a controlled environment which, to the greatest degree possible, insures the material's continued preservation without unduly discouraging its use.

A controlled environment in the reference process entails regulations concerning how the repository's material will be used as well as the regulation of the patron's behavior itself. The fundamental restriction on use integral to the concept of an archival or research collection is the non-circulating, non-browsing nature of the collections. It is this policy which allows the archives staff to control the conditions under which the collections are handled. Patrons' only access to materials should be in a supervised reading room. Unsupervised access to an archives collections should not occur.

With the ability to control access, the repository gains the ability to specify how the material will be used. These specifications should be codified in a reading room policy given to each patron. This policy should state the repository's regulations concerning such things as the proper handling of the materials, what writing implements are allowed at the reference table, and policies relating to duplication, retrieval of materials, and proper method of citation. The reading room policy should also include a statement denying the researcher access to materials if he or she does not comply with the regulations.

The above relate specifically to rules concerning the physical use of archival materials. Academic archivists must also wrestle with the problems of access to unpublished primary source material. Access undeniably is the very heart of archival reference service; if access is denied or limited, the reference process is skewed. Access to materials can be denied by statute, by donor request or by institutional fiat. This occurs particularly in the case of an academic archives in which state statute dictates access to state records in public universities, federal statutes dictate access to student records i.e., Buckley Amendment, or a college or university's governing authority (President, Board of Trustees, etc.) can decree a blanket time limit on access to university records (e.g., 25 years). In such instances it is not used unless legal exceptions to that restriction can be obtained.

Every academic archives should have an official policy concerning access to the institution's records. Such a policy should delineate clearly the type of records available or restricted, the rights of the patron (if any) to request access to restricted materials and the responsibilities of the repository to make available as openly as possible its archival collections. Before permission to examine records is granted, patrons should be asked to read and sign a statement indicating that they agree to abide by the policy and hold the institution or its employees blameless for any violation of copyright, donor or institutional restrictions by that patron.

LEGAL CONCEPTS

Finally, any archival reference policy must be built around two legal concepts or "permissions": permission to examine and permission to publish. Access and use in an archival facility implies only that an individual routinely will be given permission to examine the materials in that repository if all rules and regulations are adhered to. In no instance is permission to publish those materials given routinely. Reference service is based on the assumption that the patron will use those materials only for personal research. This is not to say or deny that those materials cannot be published or used commercially. It does say, however, that such use should be considered on the merits of each request. Such considerations are not part of the reference process except in as much as it is necessary to distinguish requests to examine materials from those legitimate requests to publish or commercially use those materials.

In the reference process it is not enough to identify the researcher who will be using archival materials, and it is certainly not enough to have only physical control over that material through appropriate use and access policies. The most important factor in a successful reference system is the intellectual control the archival staff has over the repository's material. Intellectual controls are those which facilitate the identification of the material and information sought by the researcher. The more recognizable term for this is "bibliographic control." However, since only a small percentage of an academic archives' holdings are in book form, that term does not really apply, nor does bibliographic control sufficiently indicate the wide variety of controls necessary to facilitate access to the types of materials found in an archival or manuscript collection, e.g., manuscripts, books, pamphlets, photographs, maps, A-V material, oral histories, etc.

Intellectual controls should be designed and developed with the following criteria in mind: the type of patron using the materials, the amount of use that material receives, and the nature of the material itself.

In terms of intellectual control there is almost no limit to the time and effort one can expend in describing and "intellectually controlling" archival material. Because no academic archives is blessed with unlimited time, staff or budget, however, the trick is to match the appropriate level of detail or intellectual control with the various materials in the archives. To illustrate this process, I will evaluate by the criteria listed above the following materials found in any academic archives: the student newspaper, institutional records, and photographs.

The student newspaper at any college or university, as imperfect as it may be, is generally the most complete and understandable record of college life. It provides an unbroken, if subjective, chronology of the people, events and decisions of its institution. The constituency using the student newspaper will include all patron groups of the archives. It will, however, be used predominantly by undergraduates. Of all the archives materials, it will be the most familiar and understandable to them and will be the appropriate source for the level of research for the majority of their projects. In terms of use, experience has shown that invariably it is either the most heavily used item or close to it. The nature of a newspaper is well-known. It is serial in nature and includes a great deal of information organized more by editorial decision than by the subject of that information. Finally, research in any newspapers, large or small, is not easily done without the creation of an index—itself a time-consuming and labor-intensive process.

In my experience and opinion, the importance of the student newspaper as a historic source and the great deal of use it receives, outweigh the heavy commitment of time and staff to producing an index. Since the only alternative is a non-indexed source which can be used only by perusing issue by issue, the evaluation by the three criteria indicates a clear case for a commitment to a long-term indexing project.

A college or university archives exists to acquire, preserve and make available its institution's non-current records of archival value. These records will not only be a repository's most valuable materials but will also be the most voluminous and most time-consuming to process. The detail to which these records are described will to a great extent determine how the archival staff will spend their time. In applying the three criteria to institutional records, one finds there are two major constituencies: the serious researcher for whom primary source material is the main component of any qualitative study and the administrative staff of the institution for whom these are, after all, the college's "old" records.

INSTITUTIONAL RECORDS

Institutional records, although the most important records in an archives, are rarely the most heavily-used materials. Generally their use falls in the mid-range quantitatively. Additionally, my experience has been that, of the two major groups using archival records, administrative staff use the records with greater frequency than scholars. For whatever reason, serious research concentrating on higher educational topics is still the exception rather than the rule.

Finally, the nature of modern-day institutional records revolves around their unique nature and more often than not their large volume. Archival records from significant offices on campus can easily run from 25 linear feet to well over 100 linear feet. Equally it is true that institutional records are more important in the whole than when taken individually. Although the records of the President's office, for example, are very important records, nevertheless not every letter or report taken singly is of importance.

These factors, when balanced by most academic archives, lead to archival finding aids based on description to no more than the folder level. This is not to say that reference tools providing item level access are impossible to produce. It says, rather, that item level description is usually out of the scope of most archives in terms of staff time available and level of use to justify such detail.

Photographs and graphic materials reproduce, capture and preserve the visual image of the institution and its people, places and events. They serve both artifactual and documentary purposes and as such can pose a dilemma for the archivist pondering how best to organize and describe them.

In my experience there is no readily discernible constituency for photographic materials. Their use in academic archives appears to be mainly illustrative, i.e., included in university publications, external publicity, commemorative exhibits, etc., although this is not always the case. For some research, there are instances when a visual image is essential. The use of photographic materials, however, is sporadic even if often very intensive. Quantitatively, photographs are used in substantial numbers over a year's period.

It is the nature of photographs themselves that causes the most difficulties for archivists in deciding just what to do with them. In an academic archives the vast majority of photographs come from university offices. A strict adherence to provenance would then keep photographs from different offices separate no matter their similarity in image. A photograph, however, unlike a single letter or document, often has an individual identity outside its record series, i.e., other photos from the originating office. In a descriptive sense a photograph can stand alone whereas individual items from office files often make little sense when removed from those files.

Similarly, photographs record specific subjects, events, places or individuals. They are taken to visually document those things and as such can stand as a complete or finished record. In other words, when identified, graphic images can stand alone as a complete primary source record without supplementary documentation. This factor can also lend some credence to the desire for item-level cataloging, a concept often considered anathema to archivists.

One method of achieving intellectual control of photographs in a university archives is to arrange them in a subject filing system regardless of provenance with some image-level description for selected images. The term image-level description is used deliberately to indicate the grouping of like images under a single heading, e.g., Dedication of Nobel Library, Founder's Day, Moving Crew. My interpretation of the three criteria has over the years led me to this system; not everyone would interpret the same criteria similarly.

SUMMARY

Intellectual control, then, in any reference system depends upon an in-depth evaluation of the user, use, and nature of the material to be controlled. The unique nature of the material itself and of the repository holding those materials insure that this type of close examination is necessary in order to develop the most appropriate finding aids and reference tools.

The average archivist can expect at least once in a career to inherit a reference system or reference tools not of his or her own making. It is also likely that each archivist during that same career will have to change drastically or abandon completely a system created by a former archivist. Indeed, new technology may demand changes in manual or even automated systems that had previously been perceived as functioning adequately.

What I have presented is my own blueprint for the evaluation of existing reference service in an academic archives or manuscript repository. My training and experience is as idiosyncratic as the next archivist's; in a profession without professional accreditation, without a standard educational background, and without any real standardization of practice or material, it is difficult not to be idiosyncratic. Nevertheless, the concept that there are standard components for reference service in any archives is valid. Although individual archives may not be able to compare specific reference tools and practices, each archives can evaluate those tools and practices in light of its specific constituencies, accepted rules and regulations regarding use and accessibility, and intellectual controls based upon the user, use and nature of the materials.

The ability of an experienced archivist to evaluate the services and practices of another archives in terms of the components presented here allows that individual to function in a profession rooted in individuality and variance. It provides the archivist a framework to decide whether indeed he can wear another's shoes or whether he should seek a better fit.

The Past in the Present: Reference in a British University Archival Collection

F. W. Ratcliffe

No aspect of service in British Archival Collections can be properly considered without reference to the historical treatment of Archives in Britain and the development of the profession of the archivist.[1] As recently as 1948 the great luminary among British archivists, Sir Hilary Jenkinson, entitled his introductory lecture to a new course in archive administration at University College, London, *The English Archivist: A New Profession.* Yet in the same lecture he observed that "we began to awake to the profit of exploiting old documents for the correction or enlargement of our ideas upon points of history and antiquities so early as the sixteenth and seventeenth centuries."[2] Dugdale and Rymer are familiar names in university libraries with a decidedly archival as well as distinctly historical background. *Magna carta* itself might convey the impression that the archival function is anything but new. Nevertheless, it is fair to say that in Britain the profession of archivist, if not the practice, is very much a post-Second World War creation.

It is often pointed out that the introduction of archives as an independent element in the information network did not come about through a conscious act of government as it did in France in 1796 but through a process of evolution. The 1838 *Act for keeping safely the Public Records* is sometimes regarded as the official beginning but there were various parliamentary enquiries into the keeping of records and government commissions before that date. In much the same way there were other Record Office measures and historical manuscripts initiatives in the century which followed, not least among them being the appointment in 1869 of the Royal Historical Manuscripts Commission. Mostly these centred on the Public

---

The author is Librarian of the Cambridge University Library, Cambridge, England. CB3 9DR.

Record Office in London. It was not until the nineteen-twenties that the Archivist rather than the Assistant Keeper of Records emerged. In 1923 the first County Record Office was established in Bedfordshire and the Law of Property Act, amended in 1924, empowered the Master of the Rolls to recognise libraries and record offices as suitable for the receipt of manorial records and other documents. From the sole official presence in the shape of the Public Record Office the situation changed to that of today where archivists are wont to complain that too many repositories exist.

Two main bodies now represent archives and archivists specifically in the country. The British Records Association, founded in 1932, and the Society of Archivists, which succeeded in 1954 the Society of Local Archivists, established seven years earlier. The latter is the professional body for Archivists, the former the focal point for most archival interests and activities. It was the initiative of the British Records Association in 1943 which was to lead to the establishment in 1945 of the National Register of Archives. In the words of Hodson this "Vast guide to Manuscript Sources has proved triumphantly successful: there is nothing comparable with it in any other country".[3] Nevertheless, given this specific organisation and explicit representation for Archives and Archivists, the Library Association has held and still holds on behalf of librarians a very positive attitude to the administration of this part of the national heritage.

The development of this new profession could only have significant implications for libraries. Archivists are not in doubt as to the primary role played by libraries. In an editorial on the occasion of the centenary celebration of the Public Libraries Act, 1850, the periodical *Archives* wrote: "While the primary duty of Public Libraries is to provide books they tend to attract to themselves a remarkable diversity of other duties—and among these is one for which they deserve particular gratitude—the charge and care of manuscripts and archives".[4] Two years earlier Jenkinson said much the same: "Historians and Archivists alike owe them [libraries] a lasting debt . . . they provided storage and custody in numerous instances . . . when no other Authorities were willing to come forward".[5] In this they were not so much far-sighted custodians of the documented past but almost accidental recipients of manuscript materials. Lt. Col. Malet, in a lecture in the John Rylands Library in 1946, noted that "in the medieval period they [archives] were kept for purely practical ends".[6] This was certainly true of the records of the landed gentry and remained so down into the present century until copyhold tenure ceased to exist. The extensive archives of the Earls of Crawford and Balcarres, hitherto unlisted, have only to be compared with the various catalogues of the Bibliotheca Lindesiana, the magnificent library of the Lindsay family. Immensely rich as the latter was, the records can be seen as hardly less interesting than the library itself.[7] Records, muniments are essentially the products of day-to-day activity, the management of the estates or private correspondence, not to be confused with the products of individual authors, whether in manuscript or in print. They were not accorded the same treatment as books in the library or manuscripts with authors, but stored away in those bundles or parcels so familiar to anyone working in archives, tied often with string or ribbon, in which they are all too often still to be found to this day.

The Public Libraries Act of 1850 indirectly constituted a powerful stimulus to archival activities as well as achieving its immediate objectives. Virtually all the new libraries took up the reference by William Ewart, in introducing the Bill, to local history and came to regard the creation of local collections as an important part of their function. Indeed, this is an area of Special Collection activity which they have made very much their own. It was an activity aided and abetted by the British practice, not shared by the European countries, of non-centralisation of local records, so that there was an abundance of readily available material. These collections extended far beyond printed books and large quantities of manuscript materials found their way into public libraries. In a Library Association survey in 1961, no less than 169 public libraries reported holding and collecting manuscripts. In many cases the collections ranged from "large" to "very large".[8] In 1968, the Library Association issued its policy statement on the place of archives in libraries. This commences, somewhat aggressively: "The acquisition of archives and manuscripts is a legitimate purpose of libraries serving the interests of scholarship and research. Such materials may be appropriately consulted alongside collections of printed books, which are often needed to supplement or elucidate the manuscript material."[9]

The same survey extended to British University libraries and revealed that most of them, if not all—since a minority failed to respond to the survey—held manuscripts, including some very large collections. This might well have been expected in view of the reference in the Library Association Policy Statement to "scholarship and research". No less unexpected is the absence by and large of public records in university library collections, that is of materials produced by government, whether local or national. For one thing they do not have the statutory obligation to collect them, unlike the County Record Offices. They may, like the latter, be recognised as official repositories for manorial records or for the British Record Association but the presence of local government official records is likely to be unintentional. The archives which are to be found, other than those records produced in the administration of the university, will almost invariably be the result of a specific decision to acquire them for their immediate or long-term research potential, as opportunity has arisen.

It will not be overlooked that university institutions, like public or other bodies, do themselves create records. The question has to be faced early in the life of such institutions how and where these are to be preserved. There is no need to elaborate on the formation of these archives: librarians will readily acknowledge that their own library administrative files grow apace. Since these represent only one aspect of the university bureaucracy, it is easy to see how these files are multiplied by other departments, apart from those of the central administration. One of the earliest uses of microforms within universities outside their libraries was to preserve and store student records. This is now giving way to on-line access as the automation picture changes.

In the case of the older and larger university it is not difficult to see that the archival situation will be both extensive and complicated. In a university such as Cambridge its archives are certain to compare at least in size and importance with those of other kinds of institutions of comparable age. In such a university an archive will have developed over the centuries though it may well never have been recognised formally and certainly not arranged as such until comparatively recent times. In Cambridge there are six centuries of recorded history in which many departments of varying sizes and innumerable distinguished individuals, scholars, literary personalities and national figures, have played a part. The national role of the University and deeply rooted involvement in the life of the town and the county add a further dimension which also provides rich archival materials. The extent and importance of this ancient archive was such that in 1972 it was transferred from the central administration to the University Library as an independent department within the Special Collections division. The Keeper of the University Archives and the Assistant Keeper became members of the University Library staff.

The reasons for this transfer are not far to seek. The expert department in any university in the storing and retrieving of information is its library. Moreover, when that library has a large special collections division, incorporating a large and significant department of manuscripts, these retrieval and storage skills will have been tailored and refined to suit precisely the requirements of the university archives. In Cambridge University Library this is exactly the case and since the Keeper of Manuscripts and most of his staff are also trained archivists as well as palaeographers in the traditional manuscript mould the logic of the transfer is all the more apparent. It underlines what many older librarians in Britain still regard as a retrograde step in the library profession, namely, the development of Archives administration as a separate profession apart from librarianship, though based on a part of library activity which to some extent represents the *raison d'etre* of librarianship. Happily the somewhat tense relationship between librarians and archivists, exhibited during the late fifties and sixties, are much less in evidence today.

The University Library in Cambridge has a well established Department of Manuscripts. The transfer of the University Archives to the Library brought into the Special Collections Division another Department with functions identical in many respects to those of the Manuscripts Department. The principal difference between them lies in the way they were formed. The Manuscripts Department reflects the research and teaching interests of the University. The University archives reflects the government of the University in all its various facets from the beginning of recorded university activity. The former is a specially created scholarly facility which, important as its provision is, must nevertheless be subject to all those pressures experienced by all departments in libraries, when staffing fails to match accessions growth and reader activity. The Archives are the product of University life and administration, an account of its origins and development, the "back files" to much current practice. Were the two departments to be merged, the Archives would understandably become subject to these same administrative delays which beset the Manuscripts and other Departments in the Library.

The similarities of the two departments extend beyond the purely manuscript or typescript nature of a large part of their contents. The fact is that the Manuscripts Department, over the years, has acquired extensive archives of one kind or another which exceed in quantity the total holdings of the University Archives by a considerable margin. Its function has not been just to acquire Western and Oriental manuscripts in the accepted and limited definition of literary or illuminated manuscripts, creative works of art and calligraphic masterpieces, those great monuments of Western and Eastern culture. Miss Renshaw, sometime Archivist in the University Library of Nottingham, summed up their role as follows: "We accept anything we are not legally debarred from receiving". Cambridge would qualify that and add, "provided it contributes to the research or teaching potential of the University Library". Nevertheless, she is speaking for many academic libraries when she writes of the policies and practices of Nottingham University Library: "Whereas the county record office usually has come into being to care for the local government records . . . the university library turns to the semi-official body and the private owner, offering to free them from the responsibility of custody if they will agree to their manuscripts being brought to the university and made easier of access to students".[10]

The size of the archival collections in the University Library of Cambridge is very large and the scope very wide. The Department of Manuscripts houses Diocesan Records, the papers of individuals such as Stanley Baldwin, Charles Darwin, Sir Samuel Hoare, Lord Kelvin, Arthur Schnitzler, family and estate papers such as the Cholmondeley (Houghton) manuscripts, those of the Marquess of Crewe, and of Lord Acton, the records of great companies such as Jardine Matheson, Phoenix Insurance and many others as numerous as they are varied. These are essentially of much the same character as the University Archives, by-products of working lives or administrative processes, not the deliberate, consciously produced literary work, creative writing. Their treatment differs from that of the University Archives Department only in the sense of immediacy and urgency of the latter. Moreover, the large number of collections in the Manuscripts Department is constantly being expanded by further large-scale additions. This is in no sense a "new" library activity but falls squarely into the Library's manuscript collection building traditions.

Whilst it is important to distinguish the two as separate departments, they work closely together wherever possible. One of the principal objectives of the transfer was to share and make use of existing facilities and expertise. The same storage, the same public reading rooms, the same retrieval staff, the same copies of works of reference for readers and staff serve both departments. The Archives also make use of all the general library services available to the Special Collections Division, whilst taking advantage of those special facilities introduced by and for the Manuscripts Department. It also follows that the Archives Department operates completely within the general rules and regulations of the Library and, further, conforms to all those additional provisions of use designed to protect all the Library's rare books and manuscripts.

Under the Ordinances of the University, use of the University Library is determined either by membership of the University or by producing evidence of an applicant's scholarly need and academic integrity. If scholarship or the scholarly nature of the enquiry are in doubt, the would-be user is not admitted. Having said that, during vacations, more non-members of the university are to be found using the research resources than members, so that the admissions policy, though rigorous, is not ungenerous. The days of casual use have long since gone. The growth in British libraries in the post-war period of loss and mutilation of materials has brought about strict reappraisals of library security measures. External users are required to apply for reader status in advance of their first visit and also to come armed with means of identification. In departments with much valuable and sensitive material the measures are that much more searching. In 1982, a leaf removed from a manuscript around 1840 was returned by a German University Library, having been found in the effects of a "benefactor". Some four years ago a large number of documents, missing from an important commercial archive, were sent back anonymously to the Library, the sender alleging that they had been removed "inadvertently" in the late 1950s. Such twinges of conscience are few: materials missing from these departments rarely find their way back to the Library. Today, the emphasis has to be on preventing such losses with all the inconveniences and apparent unhelpfulness to readers which that entails.

Much archival material, whether given to the Library or placed on deposit, arrives with special conditions of use attached. Increasingly, such accessions are the subject of written agreements, often legally executed, not infrequently imposing limitations of use to which the Library strictly adheres. For example, the diaries of the novelist Stella Benson, closed to users at her request for fifty years, were opened to researchers on 6 December 1983. During the whole of that time, the diaries had lain untouched, even to the extent that the library processing was limited to an external description of the materials. The Papers of both the Marquess of Crewe and Stanley Baldwin, who died in 1945 and 1947 respectively, were not available until 1973 and 1970, at their request. Again, the extensive records of Jardine Matheson were presented to the Library in the 1930s on the condition that the firm retain certain powers over use. This archive is regularly supplemented by additional materials and its use from the Library's point of view has been greatly assisted by this provision. The fact that a close liaison with the firm has developed can only be additionally advantageous to the University. Beyond these limitations, access to modern archives dealing with public matters is always liable to be restricted under the thirty, formerly fifty-year, rule which regulates access to public records. The Manuscripts Department is fully aware of the need to protect the interests of donors and depositors as well as its own reputation in the use of what is frequently legally and professionally sensitive material.

The Library attaches importance to agreements about deposits and gifts, not least because the former in recent years have become much more precarious. The plight of many landed families—their need for funds to assist in the maintenance of their properties—has caused not a few to reconsider deposits of papers and has led in some instances to the withdrawal of material. In general the University Library seeks to "buy in" the material since much investment will have been made in the listing of the collection in addition to expenditure incurred in storage and conservation. Ironically, in these circumstances, the handlists and reference material compiled by the Library are usually the main source of information about the content of the collection and, therefore, the instrument on which the owner and the auctioneer or valuer will rely in any contemplated sale. Usually, unless the price is prohibitively high, the possibility of the Library acquiring the collection at an advantageous price is fairly strong. The Library recently secured the papers of the Cholmondeley (Houghton) estate, which contain among numerous other documents, the papers of Sir Robert Walpole. They had been on deposit since 1951. Most large academic libraries and County Record Offices are experiencing difficulties of this kind. In the John Rylands University Library of Manchester, the Arley Charters were transferred in Library ownership by Viscount and Lady Ashbrook in 1979, at a price which reflected the long custodianship of the papers by the Library. Just how important it is for scholarship and for the library to secure such deposits is to be seen from the Mainwaring

Papers formerly held by the Rylands Library. They were deposited by the family early in this century and dispersed by a descendant some 40 years later. Today, only the published lists of the library indicate the extent and scope of the collection formerly in its care. The researcher seeking now to use this important collection of family papers will be hard pressed to discover where all the various items are now to be found.

Agreements with cathedrals, churches, companies, societies and similar bodies are no less important. It is now recognised that whatever else, the threat of removing collections necessitates some built-in protection for the library, compensation for its undoubted investment in the collections, at the time of acceptance. There can be no doubt that deposits from all such bodies in the changed financial climate of today are just as vulnerable to disposal as those made by individuals. Cathedrals, churches, societies are always in need of money: companies do go into liquidation, great industrial concerns can be "taken over". Indeed, one reason for transferring the very valuable archives of the *Manchester Guardian* into university ownership within the John Rylands University Library of Manchester rather than placing them on deposit was to remove the archives from any possible future interpretation as a disposable asset by liquidators. Given the disappearance of so many household newspaper titles in Britain since 1945, this step contained more realism than might originally have been supposed. The day could come when the records of a corporate body, as with those of individuals, might well be the only evidence that the company ever existed at all. That is all too true of the former cotton "giants" in Lancashire which have now disappeared almost without a trace, unless their records have been deposited in an archive or record office.

The use of all materials in the Special Collections Division is inevitably reference based. Archival materials are issued to readers with the same care as medieval manuscripts and the reading rooms are under constant surveillance by trained staff. Entry to the University Library by accredited readers necessitates the production of their reader ticket which incorporates their photograph and their bar-code. This has to be produced again on requesting any materials in the Special Collections Division and ensures a double check in the Manuscripts Reading Room where archives must be used. Items may not be removed from the Reading Room for study elsewhere in the Library and all items, even if required the following day, must be returned to the issue desk when the Reading Room closes. Strict limits are imposed on the number of items issued at one time and each item is checked individually both on issue and return. The work rooms are situated to the rear of the issue desk and the Reading Room is never left unsupervised. Microform reading equipment and similar aids are available in the immediate area so that it is never necessary for materials to leave the Room except for Library purposes. Books and microforms from other parts of the Library can be brought to the Room for consultation alongside the manuscript materials, delivered by library staff should they be part of the closed access collections. The only elements of open access in this area are the printed works of reference relating to manuscripts and archives which are housed within the Reading Room.

The statistics of use are difficult to interpret, if only because of the academic standing of the individuals and the advanced nature of their research. The average number of users signing the visitors' book over the last four years stands at around 500 a year. The current number of items produced annually exceeds 13,000 and the total of postal enquiries answered positively rarely falls below 600, of which at least half will be from overseas. Photocopies, microfilms and other forms of photographic reproduction run currently at around 22,000 per annum, to which are to be added those produced for commercial facsimile publication. The latter activity has increased significantly in recent time, to an extent that it brings in valuable income. It is not possible from existing reader records to identify those using archives within the Manuscripts Department but they represent a significant proportion. The separate statistics for the University Archives are of little assistance, since their use is highly specialised, almost predictable. Moreover, the University's interest in and use of its archives in the course of administering the University is a distorting factor if any comparison were to be attempted.

There is a variety of finding aids available to users, such as the Accessions Register, an author card-index, a subject catalogue and a variety of handlists. A principal objective of the Manuscripts Department is to publish catalogues and lists which make the resources known in the widest possible way. There is a long history of such publications by the Library. Although many inventories appeared much earlier—the earliest preserved one dates from 1473 and is to be found significantly in the University Archives—the first major publication appeared during 1856-67 in five volumes.[11] Since then many publications have been issued. The handlisting of collections is a continuing process, as old as the Library, and it provides the main day-to-day means of access to the archival resources. All such handlists are eventually published, but the extent of the collections and new financial pressures are hardly conducive to a regular publishing programme. The *Summary Guide* to post-1867 accessions[12] gives some indication of the size of the problem.

The nature of the service is, indeed has to be, personal in view of the necessary security measures. Because of the type of enquiry it is also a service where far more direct assistance with the subject matter is both expected and given. A large number of enquiries satisfied by reference librarians depend on a thorough knowledge of the reference works available, on an understanding of the library's own systems and on the ability to direct to the appropriate subject specialist. In the use of manuscripts and archives much more practical help is often sought and more insight by staff into the individual holding assumed. Only the Rare Printed Books department in the Library is likely to experience similar scholarly expectations over a wide subject range but not on the same scale. The status of "expert", which clings perhaps more closely to palaeographers and archivists than to any other library staff, is one reason why the separate profession of archivist developed. Having said that, the way the University Archives have become an integral part of the Special Collections Division in Cambridge suggests that separation was not in itself a necessity.

The use of automated techniques in dealing with archives reflects the growth and popularity of these aids in the Library generally. For example, the introduction of an on-line short title catalogue of post-1978 accessions has been so successful as to change even the attitude of the cataloguing department to the traditional catalogue. Contrary to expectations, there has been no difficulty in persuading the Special Collections Division to use these techniques, rather the reverse. One imminent development will affect directly the issue of materials in the Division. The introduction of an on-line issue system, using the reader's ticket, will extend to all items issued for reference as well as to stock borrowable from the Library. Issues of archival material in the Manuscripts Reading Room will be eventually incorporated into the system. Apart from the increased efficiency in transactions it will enable much more statistical information on materials used to be provided. It will also enhance security by making available information about users' interests and their manuscript requirements.

In fact, automation is particularly well suited to the needs of the

Special Collections Division, which deals frequently with self-contained, closed collections of materials. This is particularly true of archives and listing will eventually be done entirely via the keyboard. There are other aspects which are perhaps even more far-reaching. For example, the Library's Darwin Collection is without doubt the largest and most significant to be found anywhere, either here or abroad. The archive comprises very many thousands of items and the clientele is truly international. So great is the pressure from users that one member of staff is employed virtually full-time on sorting, dating and listing the collection, whilst being of invaluable assistance to the numerous scholars visiting the collection in the reading, identifying and interpreting of material. In the course of these activities he has achieved distinction as a Darwinian scholar and is himself much involved in the publication of *The Collected Letters of Charles Darwin*, which is based on the Library. At the same time he is also participating in the editing of Darwin's "theoretical notebook", a joint Anglo-American venture. Both enterprises have made significant use of automated techniques: in both cases the texts will be on-line from the data-bases which have been created.

Until the beginning of this century all manuscripts, whether Western or Oriental, were treated alike, as one group. This is no longer the case. The oriental manuscripts are now in the care of the Oriental and Other Languages Department which also forms part of the Special Collections Division. As a result, one of the most famous archives of the University Library is in neither the Manuscripts nor Archives Department. At the end of the last century, the Library acquired 140,000 manuscript fragments from the Ben Ezra Synagogue in Old Cairo. This repository, amassed from the tenth century onwards, contains sacred, liturgical, literary, legal, social and many other kinds of documents. The archives are a unique record of the continuing existence of a Jewish Community for nearly 1,000 years and its importance to Judaica can only be compared to that of the Dead Sea Scrolls. It attracts scholars from all over the world and the staff have made numerous contributions to the research which it has stimulated. It is of interest for another reason. Archivists have always paid much more attention to preservation than librarians have. In the current concern about conservation in Britain, it is clear that librarians have much to learn from their sister profession. In the case of the Cairo Genizah Collection, much pioneer conservation work on special materials has been carried out successfully which will benefit archivists also. The conservation awareness in the Library is due in no small measure to the successful completion of the conservation of this huge collection. All processing on the Genizah has been carried out on its own computer terminal adding a further dimension to the potential of this unique data-base for research.

In archives of such a wide range of subject interests, it is impossible to give any valid indication as to the kind of questions asked. Ecclesiastical records are as likely to promote questions as to whether certain Faculties have been granted as records of insurance companies are as to the first instance of this or that claim. As a fact, the enquiries usually relate to larger issues of scholarship and form part of some particular study. Genealogical requests are discouraged even in the University Archives where a family's belief—and it is often nothing more than that—that a previous generation has been distinguished by having an offspring at the University often leads to an enquiry. The Division is not staffed to deal with the casual or unscholarly enquiry and uses its slender resources to further the researches of those likely to be making a contribution to scholarship.

The Library's exhibition programme inevitably includes much material deriving from both the University Archives and those of the Manuscripts Department. The fiftieth anniversary of the Library's move into its present building prompted two exhibitions, one dealing with the planning and opening of the Library, the other presenting the University and the world 500 years ago. Again, in the exhibition celebrating the five-hundredth anniversary of Martin Luther's birth, in addition to letters written by Reformers, the University record of the cost of refreshments enjoyed during the public burning of Reformation Books was put on display. At least one exhibition a year derives entirely from the University Archives. This attracts many visitors and leads to many University enquiries. It also manages to generate from some quarter or other additional materials to be added either to the University Archives or to those in the Manuscripts Department. Many such exhibitions are accompanied by lectures from the Library staff. These are additional to those normally given during the academic year, in the context of teaching or post-graduate seminars. An important contribution to the scholarship of the University is made by the staff of the Archives and Manuscripts Department in their many lecturing commitments. Such lectures can be instrumental in attracting young academics to the Library staff as well as demonstrating to the University and the world outside the range of scholarship to be found on the Library staff.

The use of archives held by university libraries, their accessibility, has sometimes been a bone of contention between archivists and librarians. County record offices and public libraries often interpret numbers working on collections as evidence of a successful service. As the archives profession has grown, so too have the numbers working in record offices and in the archives held by Public Libraries. Use of original documents by the old and the young has been encouraged in these repositories and has thrived in the democratic atmosphere of a society in which education has been promoted intensively at all levels.[13] Such attitudes are quite at variance with those in university libraries, which do not use those criteria for success, and their refusal to admit "all and sundry" in the same way has produced reactions from archivists which are critical to say the least. Apart from the conservation problems aggravated by this kind of access to records, the possibility of any worthwhile research from such users is remote. The fact that libraries, having been established so much earlier, possess some very important records, simply because they were there to receive them, has been resented by many archivists and the "inaccessibility" of these records in their terms has been a favourite "whipping boy". There is no possibility of university attitudes to the use of original archival material changing. On the contrary, given some of the problems of security referred to earlier, access is likely to be restricted further, not opened to a wider circle of users.

The different attitudes and standards of use in academic libraries, the commitment to university teaching and research in university libraries, the "open door" policy in public libraries and their special status in local history, the undoubted expertise and near missionary zeal of the archivist in record offices all suggest widely differing levels of service and orders of priority. The need for all those parties to work together is of the utmost importance and quite dramatic advances in documenting the past could be achieved if the huge amount of common ground could be properly cultivated. The answer lies not in rival bodies but in one single Library and Archives Association. Until this unlikely event comes to pass, reference in archives will have many different meanings and standards for all concerned. In the meantime, co-operation is improving and seems to point the way forward. The start already made in the field of conservation may well convey to all parties that they have much to learn from each other and that common cause can only promote the interests of the reader.

NOTES

1. For a detailed account *see* Hodson, J. H. *The Administration of Archives*. Oxford: Permagon Press, 1972; for a summary description by a librarian *see* Ratcliffe, F.W. "Archival Responsibilities of University Libraries". *Journal of Librarianship* 12(1980): 71-83. The standard work on archives remains Sir H. Jenkinson's *Manual of Archive Administration*, revised second edition. London: Lund, Humphries, 1965.

2. Sir H. Jenkinson. *The English Archivist: a New Profession*. London: H. K. Lewis, 1948, p. 11.

3. *Op. cit.*, p. 26.

4. *Archives* 1:4(1950): 1.

5. *Op. cit.*, p. 12.

6. G. E. G. Malet. "The Aims and Methods of the National Register of Archives". *Bulletin of the John Rylands Library* 30(1976): 179.

7. See F. Taylor & G. A. Matheson. *Hand-list of Personal Papers from the Muniments of the Earl of Crawford and Balcarres Deposited in the John Rylands University Library of Manchester*. Manchester: The Library, 1976.

8. P. Hepworth. "Archives and Manuscripts in Libraries—1961". *Library Association Record* 64(1962): 269-283.

9. "The Place of Archives and Manuscripts in the Field of Librarianship". *Library Association Record* 71(1969): 15.

10. M. A. Renshaw. "A University Archive Repository". *Library Association Record* 56(1954): 76.

11. *A Catalogue of the Manuscripts Preserved in the Library of the University of Cambridge*. Cambridge: University Press, 1856-67, 5 vols.

12. A. E. B. Owen. *Summary Guide to Accessions of Western Manuscripts (Other than Medieval) Since 1867*. Cambridge: University Library, 1966.

13. See F. W. Ratcliffe, *op. cit.*, pp. 78-80; *and* Department of Education and Science, *Archives and Education* (DES Education Pamphlet, no. 54), 1968.

Archival Reference at a Technical University

Elizabeth C. Stewart

Amos Eaton, a lawyer turned natural philosopher, established Rensselaer Polytechnic Institute (RPI) in 1824 to instruct the sons and daughters of farmers in the "application of science to the common purposes of life". While this act was a milestone in the history of engineering education, RPI's archivists are constantly challenged to have it appreciated by the academic community. Although it is the oldest existing engineering school in the country, engineers typically have little opportunity to make use of the historical record in their daily work. Thus, the challenge of reference at a technical university is not simply how to provide the service but to whom.

BACKGROUND

Situated in Troy, New York (outside of Albany), an old industrial town currently experiencing a successful revitalization, Rensselaer Polytechnic Institute's enrollment is approximately 4,700 undergraduates; 1,900 graduates (80% male and 20% female); and 1,700 faculty and staff. Academically very rigorous, "it lacks the public recognition of rivals like MIT and Caltech, but those in the know applaud RPI's superior science programs, impressive array of computer equipment, exceptional opportunities for practical experience at the undergraduate level, and the extraordinary capacity of its nascent engineers to consume large quantities of beer."[1]

RPI was late in establishing an archives program, although several historical endeavors contributed to the facility of doing so once the time was ripe. An early history of the Institute was published

---

Ms. Stewart is Institute Archivist and Head of Special Collections, Rensselaer Polytechnic Institute, Troy, NY 12181.

[1]Fiske, Edward B. *Selective Guide to Colleges*. New York: Times Books, 1983; p.344.

in 1895, with a number of later editions; a second was published in 1968; and the Institute hosted a major celebration of its 150th anniversary in 1974. RPI's most popular president, whose tenure in the 20th century spanned nearly 40 years, (and who also authored the first history), was very conscious of RPI's place in history. Still, it was not until 1976 when for the first time the Library had a building constructed specifically to house its collections that an area was set aside for the archives and special collections. However, the area functioned without full-time or professional staff and its place in the administrative hierarchy was ambiguous.

In 1981, a professional archivist was hired along with an assistant, and the archives was elevated to the status of a department, becoming one of five in the Library, on equal standing with Reference, Technical Services, Building Services and Automation. At this writing, the staffing remains the original two full-time positions, one professional and one nonprofessional, with an ever changing assortment of student assistants, interns and volunteers.

ORGANIZATION AND ARRANGEMENT OF COLLECTIONS

The Archives and Special Collections Department contains manuscript and rare book collections documenting the history of science and technology as well as archival collections. The Department's 1984 Annual Report stated that the holdings included 1,400 linear feet of archives, 162 linear feet of manuscripts and 7,000 rare books. Arrangement and cataloging of the materials incorporate both archival and library methodology. The original materials are processed by the archives staff using standard professional practices. The rare books are cataloged by Technical Services personnel with Library of Congress call numbers and subject headings. Printed matter found in manuscript collections is frequently separated and cataloged into the rare book collections.

The organization of the archival and manuscript collections within the closed stacks reflects the different phases of the department's administration. Until the time the area was formally set up in 1981, the archival collections (the majority of the holdings), were arranged hierarchically on the shelves. The manuscript collections were kept separate from the books and archival collections but kept together as a third unit. Thus when the Department was upgraded in

1981, with virtually no finding aids or call numbers, a new system could be superimposed upon it.

The new system borrows from the plan at the Massachusetts Institute of Technology Archives and Special Collections in which materials are first designated by accession numbers and then, once processed, by a final manuscript or archival collection number. A card locator file is employed to determine where the collection is on the shelves. Since rapid growth among the archival and manuscript collections was anticipated, the system had to be flexible enough to accommodate this. Because hierarchical arrangements are most appropriate for static collections, it was decided to discontinue this practice and add a locator file, which renders the order of collections in the stacks irrelevant.

The locator file is certainly the link between the reading room and the collections for this closed stack operation, but it is the finding aid system which is relied upon to give researchers the knowledge of what is there and under what conditions it might be used. The system combines the card catalog with a fuller description—either a complete finding aid for the processed collections, or a folder heading inventory list for those awaiting arrangement and description. (Some readers might question the wisdom of listing unprocessed collections in the card catalog, but the staff feel justified in this practice because of the nature of the reference use and the overwhelming backlog: 93% archives and 30% manuscript collections are unprocessed).

RESEARCH USE

Our reference service is provided over the telephone, through the mail and in person. In a normal month between 150 and 200 researchers are served. Users come from several categories: administrative staff, faculty and students, and non-campus researchers of nearly every variety. This complexion of users varies according to the time of year: staff predominate in the early part of the academic semesters, students in the latter, and faculty, staff and visitors, all summer long.

Student and faculty clientele is small, due to the solid engineering and science curriculum. Students generally use materials for one of three purposes: (1) to prepare research papers for the elective history courses offered at the Institute, especially the History of Technology; the History of Troy, New York; or Industrial Archaeology; (2) to do research for student activities; or (3) to satisfy a personal curiosity about the school or the local region.

Equally small are the numbers of history scholars who use our collections. The centennial of the Brooklyn Bridge in 1983 did bring a flood of researchers as the archives holds one of the premier collections documenting the bridge's construction. But, more recently, in spite of efforts to publicize the holdings, the numbers of hearty souls to brave this foreign campus remain a mere trickle.

The remainder of users are Institute staff and administrators. Meeting their needs has really become the primary occupation of the staff. Most archivists would concede that when one holds archival material, one's first responsibility should be to the creators. Lacking other strong competing constituencies, we are even more inclined in that direction.

The Institute offices most dependent on our resources are the fundraising, alumni, and public relations offices. They rely on us primarily for biographical information. Academic offices also contact us frequently. Their questions range from background on the school's colors to the impetus for establishing an endowment account.

Although RPI is a technical institution, clearly the large proportion of researchers are not seeking technical information. Historians are more likely to ask technical questions, but their numbers are small compared to the researcher who simply needs nontechnical administrative history. In this respect, the Institute is not very different in its application of reference service from any other academic environment.

THE REFERENCE PROCESS

Two themes prominently underly our approach to reference service. First, we consider educating our patrons to be an important part of our function. Second, we attempt to represent original research as being in a continuum with other library research. As a result of these two attitudes, we believe researchers profit from knowledge they can apply to conducting original research elsewhere. Furthermore, the image of the archival profession benefits when the public has a more educated view of original research.

These two themes underly the way a researcher is introduced to working in our department, as well as the types of reference tools we develop.

Many first-time users suffer from one of two shortcomings which hamper their research abilities: poor basic library skills and little experience with original research. Even when one encourages patrons to approach their research well prepared, one seemingly cannot avoid patrons who must be guided through nearly every step of the research process.

Researchers frequently come to us with some familiarity with basic library skills, but little command of them. Many have only a shaky facility with use of the card catalog and almost no knowledge of published reference tools. Compounding this uneasiness with the unique practices in archival institutions often leaves inexperienced researchers uncertain and unprepared. Thus, rather than having no continuity, our practices are explained in the context of familiar library habits. For instance, we incorporate selective Library of Congress subject heading cards into our catalog and explain main entry cards as being for the creator or collector of a set of papers.

Second, we encourage many new researchers to develop a research strategy using both primary and secondary sources. Many of our users approach original research without realizing that preliminary work is necessary to place the new information into context. Without this understanding, many new researchers are totally unprepared for the process of culling unassembled information. Thus, they are easily discouraged and frequently unable to develop an appropriate conceptual framework for the new information.

First time users are dealt with uniformly whether they are staff, faculty or off campus visitors. Whenever possible, they are encouraged to come in person. This enables us to give them a brief orientation to our department and the use of original materials.

The reference interview is usually quite informal, depending somewhat on the depth of the research question. Regardless of the type of user, once it is ascertained that some actual indepth research is necessary—more than the consultation of a reference book—guidelines for using the collection, such as the use of pencil, the checking of briefcases, and the photocopy practices are reviewed. Second, the mechanics of using the card catalog and its relationship to the finding aids are reviewed.

In introducing the collections to especially engaged first time users, the staff frequently takes the opportunity to expound on the novelty and the necessity of documenting science and technology. The staff's duty to document RPI's past, both for historical and administrative reasons is also stressed. Furthermore, because this responsibility is viewed in a larger perspective. The staff also collect records documenting other accomplishments of American science and engineering as well.

Institute staff are the most frequent of the collection's users; therefore, their problems are often of greater concern than others. Outstanding among these concerns are how to facilitate their research and where our responsibility for undertaking it for them begins and ends.

Facilitating staff reference and research is really a constant effort. We sense that one of the greatest reasons why staff members do not use the Archives is that it is perceived as being too much trouble: it takes too much time and effort, and often staff find other ways around locating the information they need, even if the product suffers. While we want to encourage staff use, we also want to do so in a way that is reasonable for us, given our limited resources. We have found some ways to simplify their research.

First, procedures with regard to preparation of finding aids have been reviewed. We realized that staff have little use for the background information in the scope and content note and biographical sketches. Staff are apparently most concerned with gathering as much information as quickly as possible (often to be digested by another staff member). So, for the material they are most likely to use, the recent archival collections, our priority is to have a quality inventory available as fast as possible.

The acquisition of a computer terminal a year ago has made our inventories nearly as valuable to our researchers (if not more, to some) than our laboriously prepared finding aids, complete with biographical sketch and scope and content note. The use of student assistants to type folder headings box by box directly into the terminal has meant that in almost no time we have excellent access to collections (in beautiful copy) without the costly staff time of retyping drafts. This practice certainly does not threaten the creation of a more complete finding aid in the future, however. When a collection is later finally processed, reworking the inventory will take less time, thanks to the terminal's word processing capabilities.

Second, there is an on-going struggle with the dilemma of who does the majority of the staff research, the Institute staff or the archives staff? The higher the individual is administratively, the more difficult it is to refuse such a request. Furthermore, the tougher question to answer sometimes is, should the archives staff do it? Does one want to risk losing this important clientele, or jeopardizing a weighty supporter?

We frequently wrestle over how much research to do for administrators. It seems justified to draw the line at a half day of research for an undeniable request, that is, at a Vice-President's level, or above. There are many other requests, though, that are politely, but firmly refused. Those researchers are handled routinely; they are guided through the use of reference tools, alternative sources they may not have been aware of are suggested, but they are left to pursue the research themselves.

AUTOMATION

The role of automation is increasing in the department and eventually it should have a particular effect on reference service to RPI staff. At the moment, the terminal is being used solely, albeit effectively, for its word processing capabilities in the production of preliminary inventories and finding aids. Within the next five years, the Library's on-line catalog, which is now available for the book and journal holdings, will also include a component for the archives. When this happens, anyone with access to a terminal and the campus' centralized computer system will be able to search archival finding aids. At present, nearly every office has ready access to terminals and this can surely be expected to increase in the future. Although the level of specificity to be reflected for the archival records has not been determined yet, the access will undoubtedly mean many more inquiries from RPI staff members.

Automation is also expected to reduce the amount of outreach currently done for administrators and staff. We have always viewed outreach as one of our vital roles, particularly where staff are concerned. At the present time, administrators and staff are contacted as often as possible when it is felt the department has materials appropriate to some ongoing activity or project. It is anticipated that this kind of outreach will decrease slightly when the archival database is available all over campus. Whatever time is devoted for outreach after that, will be channeled into the cultivation of other users, for instance, students or off campus scholars.

EVALUATING OUR REFERENCE SERVICE

Reference statistics are maintained on the spot and tabulated monthly. After submission to the Library Director in the Department's monthly report, they are forwarded with other information about our activities to the university administration. Among the statistics maintained are descriptions of who the users are, what type of material is used, and whether the research takes place over the phone, in person, or by mail. While the statistics are interesting, they don't gauge as well as the staff would like the variety of research questions. They merely reflect the numbers and not the amount of staff time involved in assisting with the question. In that sense, the statistics really serve only one purpose: to demonstrate who the users are and not the lengths to which the staff goes to serve them.

For internal uses, the statistics simply confirm the staff's assumptions. However, they do demonstrate to the university administration the nature of our use and that it is on the rise. More importantly to the staff, the statistics add validity to the claim that the Department is a crucial component of the university, as demonstrated by the Institute staff who rely on services. In the future, we hope to amass information which will detail the following: the frequency of first time use over others; what source lead the researchers to the archives; and finally, what is considered the biggest deterrent to future research in the archives.

Unfortunately, there is no way to account for the research that by choice is not conducted in the archives, although it might be. Once we establish that and the reasons for it, we can confirm more accurately if we are doing a satisfactory job. For instance, we perceive that many RPI offices need indepth research conducted occasionally, but can not spare their staff for that purpose. Consequently, we are considering hiring a student assistant whose time administrators can rent for just such occasions.

CONCLUSION

The question most frequently asked us by other archivists concerns our background and preparation for this highly technical environment. The fact that none of the staff here has technical training is frequently a surprise. While such schooling would often be beneficial, it certainly is not essential. Administrative records are similar regardless of the environment, particularly if the environment is academic.

Reference service at this technical university is characterized less by the presence of some researchers (staff) than by the absence of others (faculty and students). Devotion to the administrative history seems, although by default, to overshadow the far more broad responsibility for documenting science and technology. Consequently, reference service here has more in common with a pure archival environment, such as a corporate repository, than to a liberal arts university archives.

Reference practices when possible have been adapted to the nature of the clientele. Users are primarily Institute staff, inexperienced at original research. Thus, our guides have been made as "user friendly" as possible. Research time for them is sparse, so we sought ways to prevent that from becoming a hindrance.

As automation continues to alter our work patterns, we anticipate opportunities to expand our user population in other directions. We hope to find new ways to integrate our collections into the academic curriculum, thereby balancing the staff users with a more equal ratio of students and faculty. We also want to end the very parochial nature of our users and open our doors more often to out of town visitors. The impact of science and technology is so great on this world, a broader appreciation of these materials is certainly warranted.

Of Books, Manuscripts and Jars of Snakes: Reference Service in the Museum, Archives and Records Management Section, Toronto Board of Education

Susan McGrath

The Museum, Archives and Records Management Section (MARM) of the Toronto Board of Education is responsible for a diverse collection of materials documenting the history of the Toronto Board of Education from the 1840s to the present. The collection ranges from traditional sources of information such as manuscripts, publications and historical pictures to examples of material culture such as presentation silver, major works of Canadian art and jars of snakes from a 1912 science classroom. The collection supports research on the administrative history of the Board, on past and on current issues in Toronto's education, on the development of educational ideas and techniques and their introduction into the Toronto schools and on the history of individual schools. Because of the collection's richness and accessibility, it supports research on Ontario's educational history as well. At the same time, the collection captures the classroom experience of the students and teachers, and the nostalgic recollection, sometimes good, sometimes bad, of school days. Drawing on this collection, the staff of MARM serve the educational community within the Board and a research community beyond. A traditional reference service to users is supplemented by active programs to encourage knowledge of the Board's history and to actively promote the use of the collection.

Susan McGrath is the Records Manager/Historical Librarian of the Museum, Archives and Records Management Section of the Toronto Board of Education. Toronto M5T 1P6, Canada.

© 1986 by The Haworth Press, Inc. All rights reserved.

BACKGROUND

The Toronto Board of Education of which MARM is a part is one of the largest educational systems in Canada with a budget in 1984 of $362 million. Public education policies are set by twenty-six trustees elected for a three year term. The Board operates a system of one hundred and sixty-four elementary and secondary schools, attended by 75,000 pupils and employs 4800 teachers and principals and an almost equal number of support staff, including such categories as caretakers, school secretaries, administrative staff, social workers and tradespeople. With a reputation for being progressive and innovative, the Board has taken the lead in creating alternative schools, in encouraging community participation in decision-making, in establishing affirmative action and race relations programs and in developing a curriculum for women's studies, labour education and neighbourhood history. By encouraging free expression of the cultural diversity of Toronto's people, the Board has rejected a longstanding policy of cultural assimilation in favour of a policy of cultural integration.[1]

The history of the Board of Education for the City of Toronto as it is presently constituted goes back to January 1904 when the Toronto Public School Board, the Toronto Collegiate Institute Board and the Toronto Technical School Board amalgamated. Of these three boards, the Toronto Technical School Board was a recent creation, founded in 1891. The other two boards have a longer history.

The origins of the Toronto Collegiate Institute Board can be traced back through a series of legislative enactments to Upper Canada's[2] first education act passed in 1807. This Act made provision for the establishment of a grammar school in each of the districts of Upper Canada. Based on a fees system, these district grammar schools provided a secondary level of education. In York,[3] the capital of Upper Canada, the Home District Grammar School opened in June 1807. "Most of the students came from homes of the official class, the merchants or the prosperous tradesmen".[4] It is from this school and its successors that Jarvis Collegiate Institute, the oldest school in the Toronto Board of Education system, is descended.[5]

The origins of the Toronto Public School Board can also be traced back to early provincial legislation. The Common School Act of 1816 enabled the founding of elementary schools in the towns, townships and villages of Upper Canada. These schools were perceived as serving the educational needs of the poorer inhabitants of the province whereas the grammar schools educated the elite. As early as 1816, a common school was built on the east side of Bayview Avenue.[6] This area later became known as Eglinton and was eventually annexed to Toronto. It is from this early school that John Fisher Public School, the oldest elementary school in Toronto, evolved.

Although the Toronto Collegiate Institute Board had an older history than the Toronto Public School Board, it is the Toronto Public School Board that qualifies as the real parent body for the present Toronto Board of Education. The development of a system of public education that would truly meet the educational needs of the province of Ontario began, not with the secondary schools, but with the elementary schools in the 1840s. This public school system eventually realized the principles of elected trustee representation, universal and free education and compulsory school attendance. The secondary schools, however, would not experience dramatic changes and growth until after the turn of the century.

During the 1840s a great amount of educational legislation was passed, initiated by the Rev. Egerton Ryerson, the newly appointed Superintendent of Education for the province. The acts of 1847 and 1850 were especially significant in regard to the evolution of the Toronto school system. The 1847 Act brought together under one school board, the Toronto Board of Trustees for Common Schools, the fifteen school sections in the City which previously had had their own boards. The trustees on this new centralized Board were appointed by the Toronto Municipal Council. Significantly, the new legislation made attendance free. The trustees, however, had to face a major problem immediately. There was not enough money from the government grant to operate free schools and the Municipal Council refused to levy sufficient taxes. On June 30th, 1848, the trustees closed the schools for a year. This discouraging beginning, however, resulted in a new school act passed in 1850, "the Act which has been justly called the Charter of the Ontario public school system".[7] By this Act, the school board became elected and the Municipal Council became financially responsible to the school board. Although the provision of free education was no longer compulsory under the 1850 Act, the permissive aspect of the legislation enabled the Board to declare the schools free again in 1851.

In 1950, the Toronto Board of Education celebrated the centennial of its elementary school system which had begun with 1,259 students attending classes in rented quarters. The Toronto of 1850 had a population of 25,766, still predominantly British in character and Protestant in religion. For two decades previously, however, the influx of Irish immigrants had created a significant Catholic element in the community set apart not only by its religion but by its poverty. Since 1841, Roman Catholic separate schools had been eligible for a share in public funds. Although the trustees of the Common School Board had on two occasions "presented petitions couched in earnest terms, praying that all religious distinctions in the Common School System of this Province might be altogether abolished",[8] they were unable to prevent the development of a public school system imbued with Protestantism or the concurrent growth of the separate school system.

The Common School trustees were also to face in the early years a series of financial crises around the construction of school buildings, the fluctuating school attendance figures on which the provincial grant was based on the recalcitrant nature of an unsympathetic Municipal Council. Nevertheless the public school system was bound to grow partly because of the growth in the City's population through immigration and annexation of neighbouring municipalities, and the effect of compulsory school attendance laws beginning in 1871. The eventual success of public education, however, was also due to the increasing improvement in the curriculum, in school facilities and in the qualifications of the teacher. More significant still were the social and economic factors operating in the community: the desirability of education was becoming widely accepted; its advantages for upward social mobility were increasingly apparent, and the increasing prosperity of the population made it possible for families to keep their children in school.

The preservation and promotion of this educational heritage is the principal objective behind the programs offered by MARM. The celebration of significant anniversaries can have a favourable impact on such heritage programs by increasing institutional and public support. In 1984, the Board actively participated in the celebrations surrounding the City of Toronto's Sesquicentennial. While schools produced histories of their neighbourhoods and students from across the city worked together to produce *A Young People's History of Toronto*,[9] the Board established a Museum in honour of the City's 150th birthday. Many of the activities relating to "Sesqui" were supported by the Board's collection of archival and historical materials.

The collection is made up of several collections, namely, the Manuscript Collection, the Historical Collection, the Historical Picture Collection and the Artifact Collection.

The majority of the holdings in the Manuscript Collection are housed in the Records and Archives Centre in the basement of the Education Centre, the Board's administrative headquarters. The official records begin with the minutes of the first meeting of the Toronto Board of Trustees for Common Schools on November 20, 1847. The minutes are complete to January 21, 1904, the last meeting of what had by that time become the Public School Board. In addition, the collection contains the minutes of the Collegiate Institute Board from 1851 to 1904 and the Technical School Board from 1891 to 1904. Minutes of the Toronto Board of Education exist in manuscript form until June 1909 and rough minutes are available up to 1920. Also included in the collection are minutes and reports of the committees of the different founding boards and of the Toronto Board from 1864 to the present. These official records of the political arm of the school system contain a wealth of information on the history of education in Toronto, dealing with such concerns as the provision of school buildings, the introduction of kindergarten classes, corporal punishment, the education of handicapped children, military training in the schools, to name a few examples.

The collection also houses the records of Board officials representative of the administrative side of the system. The earliest items are the diaries of Rev. James Porter, Toronto's second Local Superintendent of Public Schools, kept from 1858 to 1874, which provide insight into pupils' work and performance and that of the teachers. One of the most interesting collections are the diaries of William Carr Wilkinson who served as the Board's first Truant Officer from 1872 to 1874 and as Secretary-Treasurer to the Board from 1874 to 1919. The diaries record his experiences as Truant Officer, a new position established as a result of the introduction of compulsory school atendance in 1871, and provide a first hand look at the conditions of Toronto's poor and the lives of vagrant children. A comprehensive series of officials' reports runs from 1937 to the present documenting the issues facing the school system ranging from concerns over chocolate milk to classes for new Canadians.

Recent additions to the manuscripts reflect a trend at the Board to encourage parent, student, community and employee participation in the development of policy. Examples include the papers of the Work Group on the Proposed Students' Bill of Rights (1973), the

Work Group on Multicultural Programs (1974-1976), and the Work Group on Third Language Instruction (1980-1982).

The Manuscript Collection also includes records relating to the history of individual schools within the Board. Not all of this material is housed at the Education Centre. Some of the schools take an active interest in their heritage and in these instances are encouraged to maintain their own records. A notable example is Givens Public School, which has school diaries, student registers, and discipline books dating back to 1859. In general, student records are kept in the schools. However, the Records and Archives Centre has some student records, mainly for inner city schools no longer in existence. Access to these files is restricted.

The records of school boards which were brought into the Toronto school system when the City began to annex other municipalities in the late nineteenth century are also to be found in the Manuscript Collection. A collection of the papers of the Toronto Home and School Council founded in 1916 are on permanent loan and may be used by researchers if special permission is obtained. The papers of different teachers' associations beginning in 1881 and of other employee groups round off the collection.

The major finding aid for the Manuscript Collection is a catalogue, *An Annotated Guide to the Manuscripts in the Historical Collection of the Toronto Board of Education*, published in 1977.[10] The collection has grown since then through on-going transfers of files and material from departments, schools and individuals and through donations from former students, teachers, other employees, and individuals connected with the Board. These additions are described and indexed by subject in a card catalogue. The early manuscripts in the collection have been microfilmed to provide vital records protection and to aid in preservation of the originals. Researchers are encouraged to use the microfilm.

In addition to the Manuscript Collection, MARM is responsible for a collection of published material called the Historical Collection. This collection is first and foremost made up of Board publications of approximately 2,500 volumes beginning with the Board's first report published in 1859. This report contains not only statistics for the city public schools for 1858 but a "brief narrative of the rise and progress of the City Schools, from their inception and practical commencement, in 1844, up to the present time".[11] Annual reports were subsequently published up to 1932 and then re-introduced from 1959-60 to 1969 and from 1979 to the present. The *Minutes* of the Public School Board were published annually from 1875 to 1903 when they were continued as the *Minutes* of the Board of Education. From 1889 to the present, the Board has also published a *Year Book*. These series are all available in the Historical Collection.

The Board over the years has published, in addition to these official series, a wide range of educational and curriculum materials which form a part of the Historical Collection. At present many of the Board publications are issued not only in the two official languages (English and French) but in Chinese, Greek, Italian, Polish, Portuguese, Spanish and Vietnamese. An active effort is made to acquire all current Board publications.

The Historical Collection also contains material written about the Board or of relevance to the history of education in Ontario. Writings by Board staff, for example, James L. Hughes who served as Toronto's Inspector of Public Schools from 1874 to 1914 and who was a prolific author on educational matters, as well as a poet, are in the collection.

The books in the Historical Collection are catalogued by the Board's Library Services' Cataloguing Department. The material is arranged by the Library of Congress classification system. The Cataloguing Department also index the holdings by decade and by Board authors to provide greater accessibility to the collection. Since 1977, the card catalogue has been created through an automated cataloguing support system. At present the cataloguing for the Historical Collection is being retrospectively converted to the database. When this project is completed, there are plans to introduce a computer-output microfiche catalogue to replace the card catalogue.

In addition to book material, the Historical Collection contains vertical files (approximately 850 folders) of newspaper and magazine articles about the Board arranged by subject and a similarly-arranged pamphlet collection (approximately 4,000 items) of pamphlets, brochures and printed ephemera. These files constitute an easily accessible source of data on individual schools, Board departments, special events, and aspects of the curriculum, and include extensive biographical material. A press clippings file begun in 1877 provides a view of the Board's history from the pages of the Toronto newspapers. The file contains over sixty volumes and is arranged chronologically. At present, it is kept up-to-date by the Information and Publications Department which clips the current newspapers and then transfers the originals after six months to the

Historical Collection. A broadside collection from the 1860s to the present contains approximately 1,500 items compiled of posters, invitations, election material, and other ephemera and is arranged chronologically.

The Historical Collection also has approximately 2,000 textbooks authorized for use in the schools of Ontario from 1846 to the present. Some of the early imprints in the textbook collection have been catalogued. Most of the collection, however, is arranged by subject and then by date. The textbooks are often used for display purposes.

The Historical Collection at the present time is housed in two locations, the Records and Archives Center, and the Education Centre Reference Library on the seventh floor of the Education Centre. Planning is in progress to bring the Collection together in 1985 in the Records and Archives Centre.

MARM is also responsible for the Historical Picture Collection of approximately 4,000 items housed in the Records and Archives Centre. The collection consists of photographs of school buildings, sport teams, Board occasions, concerts, classroom activities, individuals associated with the Board and class pictures. Photocopies of the originals have been made and are arranged by subject. Researchers are encouraged to use the photocopies so that the originals are preserved. In addition, there is a collection of architectural drawings and blueprints of Board schools.

The Board's Artifact Collection falls within MARM's area of responsibility. This collection of approximately 1,800 items includes furniture, paintings, portraits, sculpture, framed photographs and prints, trophies, medals, school and office equipment and other artifacts which have been identified as being of artistic or historic value. The art works constitute one of the province's most important collections by Canadian artists.

The Artifact Collection is dispersed throughout the school system. Some of the items are located in the Records and Archives Centre, others in the offices and display areas of the Education Centre. The Sesquicentennial Museum located in the old Administration Building situated behind the Education Centre also houses part of the Artifact Collection. Most of the artifacts, however, are located in the schools. Many of the valuable artifacts, particularly paintings, were presented to the schools by graduating students and by alumni and are an important part of the heritage of individual schools.

An automated inventory produced by the Board's Computer Services Department provides access to the Artifact Collection. In addition, colour slides of the artifacts are housed in the Records and Archives Centre. These slides are arranged by the physical location of the artifacts and assist the users in identifying objects of interest to them. In 1977, in celebration of the Queen's Silver Jubilee, the Archives assembled an exhibition in the Education Centre of art, furniture and memorabilia illustrative of important milestones in the development of Toronto's school system. The catalogue published for the exhibition reflects the wide variety of materials in the Artifact Collection.[12]

In order that the collections under MARM be fully utilized, the staff offer a variety of on-going programs to the Toronto Board and to the community. These programs include a records management program, a museum, field trips, fine art exhibitions, special exhibitions and school tours.

To ensure the preservation of the Board's records of administrative, legal, fiscal and historical value as well as to assist the Board's administrative departments in the identification, storage and disposition of inactive records, a records management program under MARM has been initiated. Records retention schedules established in 1961 are being revised. An automated records control system is also being considered. The inactive records which are presently stored in the Records and Archives Centre belong to the individual departments and are not available to the public.

The Museum established in honour of Toronto's Sesquicentennial is the responsibility of MARM. It occupies what was the Board room from 1917, when the old administration Building opened, to 1961 when the new Education Centre was completed. This Board Room "of distinctive architectural beauty"[13] has been restored and in its new role as an educational museum will host visiting school classes and public tours as well as provide a handsome setting for Board special events.

Since the fall of 1984 the Museum has been part of a field trip program with grade 7 and 8 students sponsored by the Board and the Enoch Turner Schoolhouse Foundation. The program is called Daily Pursuits: Life in Early Toronto and is the responsibility of MARM. The field trip consists of a morning visit to the Sesquicentennial Museum where students are introduced to nineteenth century Toronto social history through a "hands-on" experience of artifacts and other historical documents from the collections. In the afternoon, the students visit the Enoch Turner Schoolhouse, a restored 1848 schoolhouse in the old part of the City, and then tour the neighborhood around the schoolhouse, one of the City's most intact nineteenth century middle and working class neighborhoods. From November 1984 to March 1985 627 students from 30 classes have participated in the Daily Pursuits program.

The current curriculum guidelines issued by the Ontario Ministry of Education combined with the Board's concern for neighbourhoods have created a new emphasis on local history of which the Daily Pursuits program is one aspect. The City's Sesquicentennial celebrations have also increased awareness of local history. Toronto's high school students have been participating in the excavation of Fort Rouille, a small French trading post built in 1750-51, and the excavation of the site of the 1832 Upper Canada Parliament Buildings (coordinated by the Ontario Heritage Foundation). This "hands-on" learning experience for Toronto students is likely to continue. The collections administration by MARM are being increasingly utilized for support of such programs as the statistics described elsewhere in this article indicate. For example, the Ontario Heritage Foundation is presently identifying potential school sites in the Board's property papers located in the Archives for further archaeological projects involving students.

MARM also has an on-going program of fine art exhibitions selected from the school collections. The works of art are displayed in the foyer to the Board Room in the Education Centre. The exhibitions have a theme, for example, paintings of schools and neighbourhoods and Ontario landscape paintings. A catalogue is prepared to accompany the exhibits.

Special exhibitions are also mounted by the department. The Silver Jubilee Exhibition was one. Another exhibition was one in honour of Harold Menzies who served for many years as a trustee of the Board beginning in 1932.

School visits to the Records and Archives Centre and Museum are encouraged. The students are shown the collections and also receive a tour of the Education Centre complex including the old Administration Building.

The official history of MARM goes back to November 1, 1962, when the Board approved "the appointment of a Staff Committee to further the development of a museum and archives project in which to preserve and display documents, materials and furniture of an historical nature" and to budget for funds "to permit the purchase of historical documents and other related materials as and when they become available."[14] Under the responsibility of the Education Centre Reference Library, the Historical Collection was built up through a combination of purchases, acquisitions and transfers from within the Board, and donations. The Board's official records, for example, the manuscript minutes and the published *Minutes*, and the press clippings file were kept by the secretarial department of the Board now called the Administrative Services Department. Other departments such as the Academic Department, now called Curriculum, also had extensive files. The Education Centre Reference Library which offered an in-depth reference service to the Board aided Board personnel and serious researchers in their requests for information by utilizing these materials wherever they could be found. This coordinating and facilitating reference service was instrumental in the accomplishment of bringing much of the Board's historical and valuable materials together under one jurisdiction. On the one hand, the research value of the materials became more and more apparent. On the other, confidence was built up between Library personnel and the staff in other departments so that initial resistance to transferring materials to the Library diminished.

In 1978 the Records and Archives Centre, still under the Education Centre Reference Library, was established in the basement of the Education Centre to ensure that the Board's historical materials would be "maintained in satisfactory condition with appropriate security".[15] In 1984, there was both an administrative reorganization and an expansion of responsibilities and of staff. The Records and Archives Centre and the Historical Collection were transferred from the Library Services Department to the Administrative Services Department to form a section called Museum, Archives and Records Management. Staff was increased from two to five, one of whom is on contract. There is an Archivist who manages the section, an Assistant Archivist/Conservator who is responsible for the day-to-day operation of the Archives and conservation of the materials, a Records Manager/Historical Librarian who is responsible for the records management program and the Historical Collection, an Administrative Assistant who provides secretarial and office support, and an Historical Interpreter who runs the Daily Pursuits program and is responsible for the Museum displays. Additional staff assistance is obtained on an occasional employee basis and through the Board's Co-operative Education program where high school students combine their studies with paid work experience.

The resources of MARM are normally restricted to use by the trustees, and the school and administrative staff and pupils of the Toronto Board of Education. Access is also granted, upon completion of a "Registration for Research" card, to outside students and researchers.

An analysis of the user groups for 1984 is in Table 1. This breakdown identifies the school community, that is, the students, teachers and parents, as the largest user group at 68%. The teachers and students in this group use the collections for two main purposes: curriculum projects and reunions and anniversaries in the schools. Some of the parents are alumni involved with the schools' celebrations or looking for school readers and poems from their own schooldays. The school anniversaries often result in publications which have drawn heavily on the archival and pictorial resources in the collection. These publications are sometimes quite handsome, for example, the coffee-table book, *Minerva's Diary: a History of Jarvis Collegiate Institute*.[16]

The second main group of users is the community, consisting of staff researchers from other archives and libraries, local historians and genealogists. This group makes up 16% of the total number of users. Included among the community group are senior citizens who need proof of age from their student records for pension purposes.

The trustees and the administration make up 7% of the total. Although this number does not appear to be large, reference service to this group is of primary importance to MARM and takes up much staff time. Requests from the trustees and the administration may be for summaries of previous Board decisions on curriculum matters and educational finance, for historical information on individual schools, or for support materials for system-wide events such as the celebration of the opening of the first kindergarten class in a Toronto school in 1883. At the request of the Director, the Archivist prepared a publication, extremely useful for reference, on the founding dates of all the Toronto schools. Service to the departments has included such things as providing the pictures and captions for three of the teachers' appointment calendars produced by the Teaching Aids Department.

Another important group, the academic community, is also 7% of the total. The university students and professors in this group come from the Ontario Institute for studies in Education, the University of Toronto, York University, and, to a lesser degree, other parts of the country. Their topics are mainly educational but the collections are

TABLE 1

ANALYSIS OF USER GROUPS, 1984

Figures are based on the registrations for research in the reading room Records and Archives Centre.

NAME OF USER GROUP	No. of Researchers by Sub-Category	Approximate % of Total Researchers by Sub-Category	Total No. of Researchers	Total Approx. %
School Community: - students - teachers - parents	425 73 17	56% 10% 2%	515	68%
Community: - archivists, local historians, etc. - proof of age/ transcripts - genealogists	90 22 6	12% 3% 1%	118	16%
Trustees/ Administrative Staff			53	7%
Academic Community: - university students - university professors	 42 13	 5% 2%	55	7%
media			10	1%
publishers			6	1%
TOTALS			757	100%

also used for more general historical and sociological research. Published works such as Robert Stamp's *The Schools of Ontario, 1876 - 1973*[17] quotes extensively from the collection.

The last two groups, the media and the publishers, each make up 1% of the total. Although small in number, their significance in bringing publicity and recognition to the collection is enormous. For example, TV Ontario, which is Ontario's educational network, uses the Historical Picture Collection extensively for illustrative material.

The degree of reference service provided by the staff of MARM varies in relation to the category of user. Requests for information from the trustees and the senior administration are answered as fully as possible by the staff. The operating principle is to provide total reference service to this user group. In some cases, not only information in a raw form is gathered together for the user but a report is prepared. For example, the Archivist prepared "A Survey of the Toronto Board of Education's Response to the Education of Immigrants from the 1840s to the 1930s" which was used as a background paper in the 1976 publication of *We Are All Immigrants to This Place*, a major statement of the Board's policies in regard to multiculturalism.[18]

Since 1979 when the Records and Archives Centre officially opened, statistics of the number of telephone requests and visitors to the reading room have been kept. Table 2 shows the increase in the use of the collections from 1979 to 1984. The Sesquicentennial celebrations partly explain the increase in 1984 although statistics for January to March of 1985 show a significant increase from last year.

In addition to providing a reference service, MARM also provides several other services to users. Loans of materials from the collection are made to the schools for exhibition during school anniversaries and reunions. Special loans are also made to outside groups for exhibition purposes. For example, paintings from the Artifact Collection were loaned to the Agnes Etherington Art Centre, Queen's University, Kingston for the exhibition of J. W. Beatty's works in 1980.[19]

Another service provided to the schools is advice on the storage and preservation of historical materials. The staff will assist principals, school librarians and teachers responsible for school archives. In addition, similar services have been provided to other school systems interested in establishing archival collections.

TABLE 2
ANNUAL NUMBER OF REFERENCE REQUESTS, 1979 - 1984

Figures include both registration for research in the Reading Room and reference requests handled by MARM staff over the telephone.

YEAR	NUMBER OF REQUESTS	% INCREASE OVER PREVIOUS YEAR
1979	461	
1980	724	57%*
1981	788	9%
1982	818	4%
1983	929	14%
1984	1177	27%

* This dramatic increase is to be explained by the impact of the provision of adequate Reading Room space in the new Records and Archives Centre thus permitting classroom use of the collections. The Archives programme had its first full year of operation from this facility in 1980.

Because of the fact that parts of the collection are in the schools, the staff will make arrangement for specific materials to be transported to the Records and Archives Centre. In some cases, the staff will accompany the user to the schools when the requested items cannot be moved. In the preparation of Edith Firth's *Toronto in Art*,[20] this arrangement was made so that the author could view the paintings in the art collection.

At present, the reading room is located in the Records and Archives Centre. It will be moved shortly to the old Administration Building where it will be located beside the Sesquicentennial

Museum in what was the Trustees' Lounge. The staff who presently work in the Records and Archives Centre will also be moving to the old Administration Building. The storage facilities in the Records and Archives Centre will be expanded to make room for the Historical Collection and additional departmental inactive files.

Although MARM offers services and programs to the research and the local communities, its primary function is to provide support for the ongoing activities of the Toronto Board of Education. The collections provide a historical perspective for members of the Board community while the programs contribute directly to the Board's initiatives in areas such as affirmative action, labour studies and support of Toronto's neighbourhoods. Through the provision of heritage programs, displays, and reference services, MARM functions as a vital and integrated part of the Toronto Board of Education.

NOTES

1. *We Are All Immigrants to This Place: (A Look at the Toronto School System in Terms of Governance and Multiculturalism)*. Toronto: Toronto Board of Education, 1976, p. 32.

2. Upper Canada was formed in 1791 when the old province of Quebec was divided. Under the Act of Union in 1841 it was renamed Canada West. In 1867, with the union of the British North American provinces to form the Dominion of Canada it became the province of Ontario.

3. Founded as the capital in 1793 by Lt. Governor J. G. Simcoe, York was incorporated as a City in 1834 when its name was changed back to Toronto, the Indian name for the site.

4. Edith G. Firth. *The Town of York, 1793-1815: a Collection of Documents of Early Toronto*. Toronto, Champlain Society, 1962, p. lxxiv.

5. Harvey Medland. *Minerva's Diary: a History of Jarvis Collegiate Institute*. Belleville, Ont.: Mika Pub. Co., 1979, p. 15-17.

6. Patricia W. Hart. *Pioneering in North York: a History of the Borough*. Toronto: General Pub. Co., 1968, p. 103.

7. *Centennial Story: the Board of Education for the City of Toronto, 1850-1950*. Toronto: T. Nelson (Canada), 1950, p. 23.

8. Toronto Board of Education. *Report of the Past History and Present Condition of the Common or Public Schools of the City of Toronto*. Toronto: Lovell & Gibson, 1859, p. 83.

9. *A Young People's History of Toronto: a Scrapbook History of Young People in Toronto*. Toronto: Toronto Board of Education, 1985, p. 39.

10. Roy Reynolds. *An Annotated Guide to the Manuscripts in the Historical Collection of the Toronto Board of Education*. Toronto: Toronto Board of Education in co-operation with the Department of History and Philosophy, Ontario Institute for Studies in Education, 1977, p. 108.

11. T.B.E. *Report of the Past History and Present Condition*. p. 9.

12. T.B.E. *Silver Jubilee Exhibition*. Toronto: The Board, 1977, p. 20.

13. *Centennial Story*, p. 131.

14. T.B.E. *Minutes, 1962*. Toronto: The Board, 1962, p. 562.

15. T.B.E. *Minutes, 1978*. Toronto: The Board, 1978, p. 457.
16. Medland. *Minerva's Diary*. p. 203.
17. Robert M. Stamp. *The Schools of Ontario, 1876-1973*. Toronto: University of Toronto Press, 1982, p. 293.
18. *We Are All Immigrants to This Place*. p. 160.
19. Dorothy M. Farr. *J. W. Beatty, 1869-1941*. Kingston Ontario: Agnes Etherington Art Centre, Queen's University, 1981.
20. Firth. *Toronto in Art: a 150 Years Through Artists' Eyes*. Toronto: Fitzhenry and Whiteside, 1983. p. 200.

Life in the Fast Lane: Reference in a Business Archives

Cynthia G. Swank

J. Walter Thompson Company may not be familiar to most people but its products are—advertisements and commercials seen and heard around the globe for such clients as Ford, Kodak, Burger King, IBM, and Rolex. It is the world's oldest and largest advertising agency.

Five years ago senior management established an archives. Our mandate was to preserve the Company's heritage. We interpreted that mandate in a standard archives mission statement. Our purpose is to survey, appraise, collect, preserve, arrange, describe, and make available those Company materials that we deem to have archival value. Archival value means informational, administrative, legal, and fiscal worth, not just historical value. The Archives' collections document the history, operations, policies, and achievements of J. Walter Thompson Company since its founding one hundred twenty years ago.[1]

ARCHIVAL COLLECTION

The types of materials the Archives staff has collected include 1000 cubic feet of paper documents, 1000 reels of microfilmed records, 5000 slides, 10,000 photographs, 250 audio tapes, 75 artifacts, 1000 publications, and one million advertisements. All these collections will continue to increase. Last year the Archives assumed responsibility for records management and now controls over 5000 cubic feet of records stored off-site as well as 150 cubic feet of ex-employee personnel files.

The Archives exist to serve the Company. We realize that merely

---

The author is the Archivist at J. Walter Thompson Company, 466 Lexington Avenue, New York, New York 10017.

© 1986 by The Haworth Press, Inc. All rights reserved.

becoming J. Walter Thompson Company's attic will not ensure the Archives' survival. We have emphasized the Archives' usefulness to the Company's staff and management through our reference service. Of the more than 400 inquiries the Archives staff handled last year, 80% emanated from internal sources. The inquiries themselves take anywhere from ten minutes to fifty hours to answer. The average is 1.6 hours per inquiry. Most employees have neither the time nor experience to use archival materials. Thus, the staff does the research and provides the answer—it may be one word, two hundred pages of photocopies of original documents, or a six-page synopsis of our research findings.

The Archives gets two types of questions: what and why. What questions require straightforward, factual answers. For example, What were broadcast billings in 1955? Who starred on the first *Lux Radio Theatre* broadcast from Hollywood? What does the Company's trademark mean? Why questions require an interpretation of the archival records, e.g., describe the philosophy of the Company since 1916. Determine the Company's attitude towards its publics—employees, clients, and consumers. Create a history slide presentation of the Chicago Office. Design two exhibits using archival materials for the worldwide managers' meeting.

Internal users generally are those people with policy-making authority or those who deal directly with the Company's publics: stockholders, security analysts, the press, clients and potential clients. Senior management, lawyers, account managers, corporate public relations officers, the new business group, and copywriters and art directors from the creative area comprise most of the users. Service departments such as finance seldom have requests.

The Archives staff must provide fast, accurate service; deadlines must be met. The information must be correct the first time. It must be communicated well orally and in writing. The staff must be able to deal effectively with all levels of staff members—from the secretary fresh out of a New York City high school to the president of the Company. The same excellent service to Company offices around the world must be provided even when the request might be a brief telex composed by a person whose first language is not English.

The growth in the number of internal inquiries, from fewer than 40 in 1979 to more than 350 in 1984, suggests that the archives has proved its value to the corporation. Most important, the quality of the reference service has made the Archives the ultimate reference source of the Company. "It all else fails, call the Archives."[2]

OUTSIDE RESEARCHERS

Our external users, numbering 70 in 1984, are familiar to most special collections librarians, manuscript curators, and archivists. They include students, academics, authors, picture researchers, museum curators, and genealogists.[3] In order to alert these outside researchers to our existence, notices have been placed in the journals and newsletters of academic and professional organizations. We have even answered queries that appeared in *The New York Times* Sunday Book Review section and have written scholars who are working in the field of advertising history but have not yet visited the Archives. These efforts have paid off. In 1984 five researchers spent at least one week each using our archival materials. Every effort is made to accommodate those researchers who do not live along the Northeast corridor. We will provide specific information by way of a letter and/or photocopies. To those inquirers with broad topics, a brief description of the Archives and a list of the collections that are available for outside researchers is sent. The inquirer is asked to write or call for an appointment to visit the Archives.

Researchers who visit the Archives read the rules governing use of the materials and fee schedule, sign a permission to examine form, and are interviewed. The interview sometimes resembles a "third degree" if the researcher has not done the basic readings or research before attempting to use the records. The staff frequently must guide the researchers to the appropriate collections because most have had no experience using a business archives and are full of misconceptions about the types of records that are created and survive in a corporation. Although finding aids are available and researchers are encouraged to peruse them, personal guidance is still necessary. Intimate service is provided both literally and figuratively. A researcher is no more than five feet away from a staff member. The staff periodically ask researchers if the materials are proving useful. Researchers are encouraged to ask questions but the staff finds it must occasionally prohibit them from reading aloud!

POLICIES AND PROCEDURES

The archives has begun to charge photocopying fees. The time spent in walking to the photocopier and copying oversize materials is worth more than the nominal fee charged. Moreover, the staff hopes to discourage the wholesale photocopying some researchers practice. A fee is also charged for making photographic prints or photostats; negatives are not made available.

The archives follows the standard procedure of having external researchers obtain permission to publish. Unlike public repositories that have a somewhat lackadaisical attitude to granting permission for most collections, the archives staff is rigorous in the checking of quotes and citations. It has become apparent that the note-taking techniques of most researchers are dismal and their direct quotes and citations frequently inaccurate. The staff cannot alter the biases of the researchers, of course, but it can make sure that sources are quoted and cited correctly.

COPYRIGHT AND ACCESS

Business archivists have two major concerns that other archivists face less frequently—copyright and access to collections. The question of copyright is not an academic one at J. Walter Thompson Company. Clients own the copyright to the advertisements the Company possesses. Thus, whenever an outside researcher wishes a reproduction-quality print, the client company must be contacted. A publisher or museum must sign an agreement indemnifying the J. Walter Thompson Company and its client against any risks incurred from the publication. This precaution is necessary because the photographer, illustrator, or models might claim a talent use payment.[4]

After arranging and describing the materials in a particular collection, the staff determines restrictions on access. There are three levels of access—materials any user, internal or external, may see; materials that only employees may see; and materials that only the officers and directors of the holding company or their representatives may see. Unprocessed materials are automatically restricted. The archives tends to be conservative in determining access because the records contain much client information. J. Walter Thompson Company obviously does not wish its clients to be publicized unfavorably or proprietary information made available to its clients' competitors.

The staff has discovered that while it must restrict access to certain records, some information in these same records can be made available with impunity. Researchers often request innocuous information. Unfortunately, however, the information might be in a restricted collection. For instance, our Radio-Television Department records are restricted because they contain contractual information about many celebrities. The staff will use the collection to provide a researcher with some information in the records, e.g., the date and stars of a particular *Kraft Music Hall* broadcast. The staff keeps track of such uses of restricted collections so that it can be sure it is providing information on an equitable basis.[5]

PROCESSING THE RECORDS

All materials are accessioned promptly. The accession record assigns a unique number to the materials and provides the donor's name and department or address, the size of the accession, and a description. If the accessioned materials consist of a carton of textual records, a list of the folder headings is prepared. Once materials are arranged—something that unfortunately might not happen for years—a finding aid that consists of a history and description of the records, their provenance, size, and container list is prepared. The finding aid also indicates what other collections might contain related information. In some cases, there are indexes, but there is no card catalogue.

The Archives has not only survived but thrived in the past five years. Its success, however, has produced strains. A time study performed last summer showed that reference, accessioning, exhibits, and records management take up virtually all the staff time. These jobs, and especially reference, have definite deadlines or must be done immediately. Processing, on the other hand, is the one task that can be put off. The long-term consequences are serious because access becomes difficult and too much information remains in the heads of long-time employees.

Accessioned but unprocessed materials have increased dramatically since Company records stored in an off-site warehouse were surveyed. Of the 6000 boxes appraised, 200 contained archival materials. It has become very time-consuming to have to plow through accession records in order to find the materials needed to answer an inquiry. The staff is in the process of evaluating the accessions to determine which ones can be combined to comprise a record group or sub-group and which ones can be joined to form artificial collections. It also expects to deaccession some materials and weed out multiple copies. The next step will be to determine the priority in which the accessions are processed.

In order to improve access to the processed collections as well as the accessions, the staff expects to develop an automated system in the near future using keywords and full text searching of finding aids. The automated system probably will be created in-house although there are some commercial programs available that might be adapted for use.

EVALUATION

The Archives not only collects paper but creates its own. For instance, the staff compiles monthly and annual reference statistics. We know how many users we have had; who they were and from what department, office, or institution; the length of time spent answering the inquiry; and the number of photocopies, photographs, or slides made. The purpose of the inquiry, e.g., new business, legal, speech or article, publicity can also be determined. It is possible to go back to the individual inquiry form and learn the exact question and the collections used to answer the query. Thus the staff does not have to research the same question again and saves time.

At the end of every year a list of our achievements is prepared. Inquiries make up one category. Other sections include number of accessions and from what departments; number of collections processed, described in terms of cubic feet; number of photographs, advertisements, and books conserved; exhibits designed and installed; slide presentations created and given; administrative achievements such as a disaster plan and procedures manual; and extra curricular activities. All these statistics help substantiate the Archives' worth to the corporation.

The Archives' real asset, however, is its people. The reference service the staff provides ensures the Archives' visibility and viability. Working in a business archives is not a back-room job. A business archivist must communicate well, recognize the purpose and priorities of the Archives, and be naturally curious and conscientious. Understanding the historical process is necessary but knowing historical facts is not. A person who is widely-read can add immeasurably to the success of a business archives. The archives training programs so many universities are now offering may provide the basics relating to the accessioning and processing of materials. The mass vital requirement, however, is to hire individuals who can handle all aspects of reference well since reference can make or break a business archives.

NOTES

1. Descriptions of standard archival policies and procedures can be found in the following publications:

> Mid-Atlantic Regional Archives Conference (MARAC). *Guidelines for Archives and Manuscript Repositories*. (New York: MARAC, 1983.)
> Society of American Archivists (SAA). *Basic Manual Series I* (Chicago: SAA, 1977).

Also: at least three SAA professional affinity sections—business archives, college and university archives, and religious archives—have established guidelines that outline institutional policies and procedures.

2. The Archives is a separate department in Corporate Administration and reports to the Assistant Secretary of the Corporation. This location in the corporate structure undoubtedly affects the support the Archives receives, e.g., the Archives was the first department included in the Company's electronic mail system.

3. Seventy researchers may seem small. Most general historical inquiries are handled by the Public Relations Department, which sends out press kits containing a brief history of the Company and a chronology of Company events that the Archives created.

4. The Archives, not the Legal Department, initiates legal review of archival policies and procedures. The Legal Department treats the Archives staff as professionals and almost always accepts their recommendations with only minor changes.

5. For descriptions of archival access policies, see:

> SAA, "American Library Association-Society of American Archivists joint Statement on Access to Original Research Materials in Libraries, Archives and Manuscript Repositories," *American Archivist* 42:4 (October 1979): 536-38.
> SAA. "Standards for Access to Research Materials in Archival and Manuscript Repositories," *American Archivist* 37:1 (January 1974): 153-54.

Researching the Past: An Archivist's Perspective

Frank A. Zabrosky

INTRODUCTION

Through the past centuries public, private, and governmental institutional libraries have been acquiring and preserving the recorded human experiences of the past, generally with emphasis on the printed record. It has been, however, only in the past three decades that there has been a dramatic expansion in the creation of archival or manuscript agencies by government, private institutions and associations, business, and the academy to gather and preserve the non-print records of historical, research, and information value.

A number of new archival centers have been established at universities and colleges in the past two decades with a primary task of collecting records and manuscripts of a traditional and non-traditional nature to enable the historian, researcher, and student to study and interpret urban industrial society in the nineteenth and twentieth centuries. The genesis of these centers was from the innovative historical interpretative approaches proposed by historians as well as from the availability of new technological aids.

The acquisitions and preservation of historical documents and records, their organization and description, and the provision for their bibliographic control might appear as ends in themselves and in the providing for intellectual access to its collections, an archival or manuscript repository might seem to express the important, if not the essential, aspect of its raison d'etre. It is, however, in the utilization and exploitation of materials to respond to the scholar's scrutiny, the student's search, the generalist's quest, and to the inquiry of the curious by which the ultimate value of a collecting agency is measured. It is herein that lie the thrill, the reward, and the frustration for the archivist as a reference facilitator.

The author is Curator, Archives of Industrial Society, at the University of Pittsburgh, Pittsburgh, Pennsylvania 15260.

© 1986 by The Haworth Press, Inc. All rights reserved.

Since it is immaterial, generally, to a patron how his inquiry might be resolved, the diversity, and at times the vastness, of historical materials originating from various sources, held in various places, described at various levels, and accessible through various means add complexity to reference service in an archives or manuscript repository. It is with analysis and synthesis that an archivist meets the reference inquiry; it is frequently through insight and random intellectual linkages which reflect an individual archivist's personal experience that a reference inquiry is matched.

ARCHIVES OF INDUSTRIAL SOCIETY

The lack of documentary resources and archival programs in Pittsburgh's public, private, educational and governmental institutions and agencies for preserving the records and documents of late nineteenth and twentieth century as represented in Pittsburgh and Western Pennsylvania provided the impetus for the development of the Archives of Industrial Society. The Archives of Industrial Society, a unit within the University of Pittsburgh Library System, is a repository for historical records and manuscripts of the late nineteenth and twentieth centuries relating primarily to Pittsburgh and secondarily to twelve counties in Southwestern Pennsylvania. While the priority and emphasis of the collecting program has been on local historical records and manuscripts, there has been a notable exception. In 1975, the University of Pittsburgh entered into an agreement with the United Electrical, Radio and Machine Workers of America (UE) whereby the Archives of Industrial Society was designated the official repository of that labor organization's archives.

Historical Note

In 1963, the Archives of Industrial Society was established at the University of Pittsburgh by the Department of History to collect and preserve records concerning the development of an industrial society with an emphasis on Pittsburgh and Western Pennsylvania. This aim was to be "a part of the broader goal of the University of Pittsburgh to study and analyze the history, present impact, and future of industrial society in a global scope." In 1966, an agreement was reached between the University Library and the Department of

History whereby the Archives of Industrial Society was to "be developed as a part of the University Library Program." With the completion in 1968 of the university's research facility, the Hillman Library, the offices and collections of AIS were moved to the Hillman Library and became a part of the University of Pittsburgh Libraries. It was not, however, until July 1, 1979, when the staff of the Archives of Industrial Society was transferred from the administrative control of the Department of History to that of the University Libraries, that a complete integration of the Archives of Industrial Society within the library system was accomplished.

Collections

The records generated in a modern urban industrialized society are numerous and varied. They spring from the political, social, economic, and cultural aspects of life in such a society and reflect the historical processes, in addition to urbanization and industrialization to those of modernization, centralization, specialization, professionalization, and bureaucratization. They originate in the individual and institutional response, which may be one of integration, conflict, or alienation, to social change. Institutional, organizational, business, and public records as well as the personal papers of individuals from multiple social sectors provide the raw data for the study, analysis, and interpretation of the social, political, economic, labor and ethnic history of nineteenth and twentieth century industrial society in Pittsburgh and Western Pennsylvania. Clusters of records reflecting public, private, organizational, and institutional aspects of modern society have been developed by the Archives and nuclei of materials emphasizing labor and working class history, political and social activism, politics and government have been fashioned.

At the end of the 1983/84 annual report period there were in the Archives some 429 ms. groups totaling 8,673 lin. ft. of documents, 1,642 microtext items, 668 cassettes, approximately 70,000 glass plates, negatives and photographic prints, and 1,861 reels of 16mm film (video footage). The Oakland Campus of the University of Pittsburgh Libraries at which the Archives is sited held, at the end of 1982/83 report period for which the last complete holdings picture was available at this writing, some 2,719,275 physical volumes of books and serials, 1,728,445 in microform units, and 313,454 government (federal, state, international) documents.

Since the Archives is physically housed in the Hillman Library, the central research facility, the Archives staff and patrons have ready access to a rich resource of specialized bibliographies, indexes, newspapers, periodicals, government documents, annual reports, directories, blue books, social registers, plat books, maps, yearbooks, publications of historical societies, etc. The main library's microtext holdings contain a vast array of original and primary source material. The library's participation in the OCLC bibliographic utility provides the capability for on-line searching of the data bases of that utility and the library's membership in the Center for Research Libraries provides access to the Center's resources.

Patrons

Scholars, students, the independent researcher, the genealogist, the interested citizen from the area, region, and nation have utilized the Archives; there have been, in addition, international contacts. The University of Pittsburgh Library System, unto the present, has had an open access policy and has served other than members of its own faculty, student body, and staff.

Any individual, including the private citizen, may enter the library and use the materials within the confines of the library but the library materials cannot be borrowed for home use; a contribution of an annual gift to the library of $25, however, provides the opportunity for an individual to join the support group, Friends of the Library, and this status affords the individual borrowing privileges for circulating items. In addition, the University of Pittsburgh, including its libraries, has reciprocal agreements with other area academic institutions which enable faculty and students from those institutions to use the University of Pittsburgh Library System as special patrons.

While the Archives will allow access to its collections and materials by all users from the academic, public, and private sectors, use is subject to special conditions and procedures. Materials from the archives collections must be used in a special reading room where use is monitored by an attendant. The patron is cautioned not to disturb the arrangement of the papers but is asked to point out to the staff what appears to be errors in the arrangement. All notes must be taken in pencil or by typewriter and the use of pens or markers is prohibited. Photocopying of materials is done by the staff and is made available for research purposes only. Permission to publish manuscripts must be specifically requested and permission granted before publication; it falls upon the researcher to secure permission to publish when that right does not lie within the Archives' purview. Patrons are provided with a statement outlining the conditions for the use of manuscripts when they wish to have access to archival materials. In addition, the Archives require the completion of a form which documents the request for permission to consult materials in the archives and embedded in this form is a paragraph, which it is hoped, sensitizes the user for a concern over the private rights of others. The paragraph, in part, reads

> I recognize my responsibility under the laws of defamation and invasion of privacy. To the extent such laws may apply, I agree not to disseminate or otherwise communicate information obtained from these materials that I know or believe (1) to be defamatory or derogatory to the reputation of any person, or (2) to constitute an invasion of privacy, or (3) to be prejudicial to the security of any person. I will not quote from these materials, either in whole or in part, without express written permission of the (designated authority).

There are some collections in the archives which have restricted or limited access and use; these conditions may have been imposed by the donor or by the archives, itself. In one instance, while the National Council of Jewish Women (Pittsburgh Section) permits a user to listen to the oral history tapes in its deposited collection and to take notes, the donor does not permit duplication of a tape nor the photocopying of the transcription of the interview. The Archives itself has applied a limited access policy to some series, e.g., police dockets and prison records which it holds. Patrons requesting access to these particular records must confer with an archives staff member. This interview provides the opportunity for the archivist to caution the patron that the user must treat the information with sensitivity since an arrest docket, while documenting that an individual was arrested, may or may not reflect the final disposition of the case or attest to either the guilt or innocence of the individual. During the last two decades, archivists and manuscript curators have become more concerned about the privacy of rights and the invasion of such rights. If any restrictions on access or use are employed, the restrictions should be applied uniformly and a rational explanation provided for the adoption of such measures.

User Profile

One of the most perplexing problems in the reference service area is that of determining the type of patron use of archival materials. In order to attempt to determine the use characteristics of patrons, the AIS initiated in November 1982 a coding system which was thought might provide use data. Categories, admittedly inperfect, were developed and expanded to include:

- A   Academic research (post-doctoral), e.g., those doing scholarly research for books, journal articles, lecture forums, etc.
  EXAMPLE: Research being done for a biography on Father Charles Owen Rice, a social and labor activist priest in Pittsburgh from the 1930s to the 1970s; researcher has a contract with a publisher.

- AR   Applied research (generally, those outside the academic community), e.g., research for use in newspapers, journals, newsletters, books, television shows, radio programs, exhibits, class lectures, etc.
  EXAMPLES: "From Slaves to Statesmen . . . a history of Blacks in Pittsburgh," article by Jerry Byrd published in *Pittsburgh Press* 10/17/82. Loan of film on Philip Murray from Rice Papers to ABC-TV for its "Close-UP" TV program.

- DTS   Dissertations, theses, and seminar papers (graduate level research, including undergraduate in-depth seminar papers).

- G   Genealogical Research, e.g., use of church records, marriage returns, etc., family history, genealogical research.

- I   General routine information about the Archives, its activities, programs.

- S   Student use, e.g., undergraduate class assignments, high school students.

- P   Public use (general reference for personal use), e.g., plat books, building permit dockets for information on an individual's house.

Analysis of patron contact information for 1983/84 indicated that:

42% of use was for academic or instructional research, e.g., those doing scholarly research for books, journal articles, theses, dissertations, seminar papers, lectures;
28.3% of use was for genealogical or private research, e.g., use of church records, marriage returns;
27.2% of use was by those outside of the academic community for newspaper articles, newsletters, television programs, radio programs, exhibits;
2.5% of use was for general information only;
24.4% of the users were from the University of Pittsburgh; and
75.6% of the users were non-University of Pittsburgh.

THE REFERENCE INQUIRY

Character and Scope

The reference and research inquiries which the Archives receives from direct personal contact and via letter and telephone range from the simple to the very complex and from the articulate to the vague. Patrons themselves may be either naive or sophisticated in their expectations as to what data exists and in what state the information may be found. It often comes as a surprise to the novice researcher that what he desires does not exist already fully analyzed and collated but that various bits of data will have to be secured from a number of diverse services and a synthesis attempted. It comes frequently as a shock to users of church records and records of fraternal and ethnic organizations that the data is in a foreign language and not only are the documents in a foreign language but, in some instances, in other than the western alphabet. (In the Archives of Industrial Society there are materials in fourteen languages: Arabic, Croatian, German, Greek, Hungarian, Italian, Latin, Polish, Russian, Slovak, Slovenian, Ukrainian, and Yiddish). There is keen disappointment when no typed translations can be provided.

In a number of instances, an inquiry may be straightforward and answered with a minimum of effort, e.g.,

> a need for the election returns by precinct level for the mayoralty campaigns in the city of Pittsburgh from 1950-1970, the

verification that a particular residential structure was constructed in the city of Pittsburgh in either 1894 or 1895, or what was the curriculum of the academic department in Pittsburgh's Central High School in 1960.

Increased reference guidance must be offered in instances which a presupposed historical knowledge does not exist, e.g.,

the physical development and change of a particular area over a 100 year period of time (in the instance of Pittsburgh, annexations and ward changes compound the complexity of the problem),

the ethnic composition of the city of Pittsburgh from 1880 to 1940 with particular reference to those immigrants from eastern and southeastern Europe (at issue here is the stage of historical evolution of the political states in Europe at any particular time and the consistency/inconsistency of the information elicited during the decennial census enumeration,

what were the zoning regulations in the city of Pittsburgh before 1900? (In Pittsburgh the Zoning Board was created only in 1921.)

Questions which require the most individualized references service center on such requests as,

What really was it like to be an immigrant in Pittsburgh during the closing decades of the 19th century?

What were the conditions under which individuals labored in the factories and mines of Western Pennsylvania during the inter-war period and what did this struggle to survive entail?

Who was Father Cox and why did he, a Catholic priest from Pittsburgh, enter the presidential campaign in 1932 as the candidate of the Blue Shirt Party?

What was the reality of the 1960s and 1970s in Pittsburgh, that era of opposition to the war in Vietnam, draft and war resistance, political protest, and formation of a peace and freedom movement?

What were the housing conditions of Pittsburgh's laboring classes between 1865-1910?

Capital punishment as it had been applied to male and female felons in Allegheny Co.

What were the sanitary conditions of Pittsburgh during the late 19th and early 20th centuries? What about street cleaning and street paving technology?

The level of need and the intricacy of the reference/research inquiry determines the track the archives staff member takes in working with a patron. The straightforward request generally will require a direct but a limited involved response; the slightly complex questions will involve more additional probing; and the intricate, an in-depth interview. The discussion which follows is limited to the methodology which is employed by the archives staff member in responding to a complex research inquiry.

Response: Strategies, Options

Successful reference service in an archives such as that represented by the Archives of Industrial Society lies in determining the level of need and providing guidance to resources which will serve that level of need. Depending on the level of need, the staff will suggest resources within the archives or the university library system as well as direct the user to resources in other libraries and repositories (local, regional, national) and to potential resources in the possession of organizations, societies, institutions, and individuals. When it is known that there are experts or knowledgeable individuals in the academic or outside community from whom leads, insights, or perspectives may be secured, these individuals are suggested as possible contacts. Obviously this approach is not undertaken indiscriminately but only after an in-depth interview has been conducted, a need clearly outlined, and an inability to respond by utilizing the known and conventional resources. This referral activity has not been only in the one direction, i.e., archives and the archivist to a particular organization or individual; students and others have been referred by the community contacts to the archives, e.g., the referral of an architect who is planning the renovation of a building for which documentary and visual proof is required before certification of historical significance can be attested. The mutual referral has proved beneficial in that services are rendered, needs are met, ties are renewed and contacts rejuvenated. When it happens that several individuals are researching an identical subject at the same time (the archives had three researchers within a matter of several weeks preparing to undertake studies on Msgr. Charles Owen Rice, a Catholic social and labor activist priest in Pittsburgh from the mid-1930s into the present), the archives will consider the option of putting the researchers in touch with one another. This is never done, however, without the prior approval of the researchers concerned.

The intricacies of a complex research inquiry are examined most successfully through an in-depth interview. Indeed, the researcher is encouraged to secure an appointment during which the scope and nature of the inquiry can be delineated. It is during this interview that the researcher can articulate a thesis, formulate a hypothesis, and explicate the research design. The interview is particularly necessary with those who are being introduced to the research exercise for the first time. All too frequently the undergraduate, even undergraduates in an honors program, and the graduate students have no real knowledge of research design or methodology and are completely unprepared for the complexity and, in instances, magnitude of the task. There has been a clear failure in academic departments and by faculty to guide and counsel the student in his or her initial research activities.

The interview is an opportunity to rectify some of that failure as well as one in which to review standard library practices, approaches, and resources with which most patrons are uninformed, and sometimes understandably so. The interview, then, becomes a teaching vehicle by which practical instruction in exploiting the collections of a research library is given.

Research libraries are complex institutions. During a particular institution's evolution, a myriad of policies, practices, and procedures has governed the type of materials acquired, their description, and their bibliographic control. Access to the vast portion of the resources which a library contains can be difficult for the knowledgeable staff member and almost impossible for the unknowing. This may be illustrated by some discussion of the holdings of the University Library System, of which the Archives of Industrial Society is a unit, at the University of Pittsburgh. This is not to suggest that the problems of bibliographic control and access are unique to that particular institution.

If one were to start and then stop with only an author, title, and subject search of the library's main card catalog, one would have been exposed only to a small proportion of the library's holdings. The limitations of the card catalog include: (1) lack of an indeterminate number of entries by title because, for a number of years prior to the mid-1960s, no title entries were inserted in the catalog;

(2) lack of analytics for several hundred thousand bibliographic entities within series which have never been analyzed or only partially analyzed (access was to be dependent on specialized bibliographies and the printed book catalogs such as that of Library of Congress, the National Union Catalog, or those for special collections within libraries, e.g., *Dictionary Catalog of the Slavonic Collections in the New York Public Library*); (3) periodicals and newspapers are not listed in the card catalog and must be approached through a printed catalog (it is true that serials information is being included in the serials data base of OCLC, but at this writing terminals for searching are generally limited, i.e., technical services area, interlibrary loan); (4) United States government documents are, for the most part, not entered in the card catalog, are arranged by the Superintendent of Documents classification notations, and are accessed through the specialized documents indexes; (5) Pennsylvania state documents, which were once classified in LC and entered in the main card catalog, have been declassified within the past several years and are now arranged by a notational scheme based on office of origin at the time the document was issued (there are, as far as I know, no printed and published checklists, catalogs, or specialized indexes/bibliographies for Pennsylvania State documents comparable to that for federal government documents); (6) municipal documents for the County of Allegheny or the City of Pittsburgh may or may not appear in the card catalog since from 1972/73 when the Urban Documents Microfiche Collection Project was begun, the library acquires copies of Allegheny County and Pittsburgh municipal documents in the microfiche format, does not enter holdings of title in that particular collection in the card catalog and relies on the *Index to Current Urban Documents* for access (most frustrating and a clear disservice is the failure to tie material entered already into the public catalog, e.g., annual reports of departments and agencies, to holdings held unclassified and in the microtext collection; in addition there has been no attempt to refer the user to the access key, *Index of Urban Documents*; (7) the main card catalog is neither a union catalog of the holdings for all libraries which may be found on its other campuses nor for all libraries on the University of Pittsburgh's Oakland Campus.

Added to the deceptiveness of inclusiveness which the card catalog masks is that of the inscrutability of what may be contained in generic titles such as annual reports, directories, proceedings, yearbooks. Only a personal past working familiarity and knowledge enables one to exploit the richness and variety of data contained in these publications: tables of statistics providing data in the ethnicity of coal miners killed in accidents at particular collieries during a given time period (Annual Reports of the Pennsylvania Inspector of Mines); reports and discussions of strikes and work stoppages in various industries during the late 19th and early 20th centuries (excerpts from case files as reported in the Annual Report of the Western Pennsylvania Humane Society under its then name of Western Pennsylvania Humane Society for the Protection of Animals, Children and Aged Persons).

The sheer volume of modern archives and manuscripts prevents calendaring, item description, or item indexing. Description is generally on a collection and series level with a series in archival terminology meaning

> File units or documents arranged in accordance with a filing system or maintained as a unit because they relate to a particular subject or function, result from the same activity, have a particular form, or because of some other relationship arising out of their creation, receipt, or use.

The series descriptions are incorporated within a written inventory which then becomes the primary access tool to particular archival record group or a manuscript group. While a departmental catalog may provide additional entry capability, detailed subject, topic, or name approaches remain a dream. Parenthetically, I do not see the new computer technology, in itself, resolving the problem. Guides to collections in other repositories, the *National Union Catalog of Manuscript Collections*, (NUCMC) the insertion of information (including all of NUCMC) in the archives and manuscript subsystems of the national bibliographic utilities of OCLC and RLIN will be a significant accomplishment for accessing archival and manuscript collections. Chadwyck-Healey's project of the *National Inventory of Documentary Sources in the United States* which promises availability in microfiche format finding aids to collections in the National Archives, the Manuscript Division of the Library of Congress and in state archives, libraries, historical societies, and academic libraries will substantially enhance the ability to provide superior reference/research service. No reputable library with aspirations to major research status will be able to sustain credibility without these tools. I look forward to the time when the University of Pittsburgh acquires these finding aids.

Case Study

Perhaps a close look at a research question which was recently handled in the archives will explicate the procedure used to address the problem, to identify potential sources of data, and to determine the location of resources.

A graduate student (M.A. program) in the history seminar was undertaking the preparation of a major research paper. This paper was to examine the causal influences of the practice of midwifery in Pittsburgh and Allegheny County particularly during the period of 1910-1930. In an interview which took place it was learned that while the 1910-1930 period was the one of emphasis, the student would be interested in material covering earlier periods; moreover, the student felt that data on infant mortality would be quite useful.

In making the appointment, the student had identified the general thrust of her research interests so it was possible prior to the appointment to think about the problem, to adopt some search strategies, and to do some preliminary searching. Prior to the interview the student had done an amount of background reading and had given extensive thought to her subject and its research design. She came to the interview with particular categories of material which she thought might be helpful, e.g., health reports, records of associations/societies, local medical/public health publications. She advised that she had checked the main public card catalog. When the interview took place, a great deal of effort on the part of both the student and the archivist had been expended, and both were prepared to look at the question.

In this instance, the discussion of potential resources was very productive since both parties had done some preliminary work. The potential sources of information identified included:

1. Annual reports of the Pittsburgh Department of Public Health, [1871/72-1916], which the Archives had previously microfilmed and now held;

2. Health records, particularly for birth and infant mortality, on deposit with the Falk Library, the medical library at the Univ. of Pittsburgh.
3. The *Pittsburgh Digest* which contained ordinances in effect at a particular time of codification;
4. Records in the possession of the Visiting Nurses Association of Pittsburgh, formerly the Public Health Association of Pittsburgh, founded in 1919;
5. Records of the Pittsburgh Academy of Medicine held by Falk Library, University of Pittsburgh;
6. Periodicals such as the *Pittsburgh Medical Journal, Pittsburgh Medical Review, Pittsburgh's Health, Social Research Bulletin* (Pittsburgh):
7. Chapter in Philip Klein's, *A Social History of Pittsburgh* (Columbia, 1938), which gave information on midwifery in Pittsburgh during the period; Klein also alluded to state certification of midwives and the allusion led to
8. Pennsylvania Laws, Statutes, etc. *State board of medical education and licensure rev. law, rules, and regulations, midwifery.* [Harrisburg, 1929]. Finding this pamphlet provided some specific dates with which newspapers, debates, etc. could be checked.
9. Identification of a professor on the staff of the School of Nursing who has had extensive experience in public health nursing and has continued her wide community and association contact.

Working on this particular question underscored the deceptiveness of the main public card catalog and the complexity of locating material of primary interest. The card catalog which the student had checked contained a subject entry for midwifes; however, a far greater number of entries dealing with midwifes could be found under the subject heading of obstetrics (there were no cross references). Under the subject heading of obstetrics, there was a card for the Pennsylvania document #8 above) giving its LC classification number. A check of the shelves, the circulation file and the storage list did not locate the item. More perplexing, there was neither a main entry nor a shelf list card; the series, however, of which this was a number appeared in the printed serials holding as a classified serial with its call number. It came as a sudden revelation that since this item was a Pennsylvania document and the Pennsylvania documents had been declassified, the item now should be found in the Pennsylvania Document Collection where, indeed, it was found. Since the arrangement of the Pennsylvania Government Document Collection is by office of origin/issuance, it was, thankfully, to the failure in withdrawing all cards, i.e., the subject entry in this instance, from the public catalog that the issuing agency, the Pennsylvania State Board of Medical Education and Licensure could be determined and the document retrieved from the Pennsylvania Government Document Collection.

The above case study puts into some perspective some of the dynamics of the reference service which is attempted in the Archives of Industrial Society. Something akin to this practice most likely occurs to an equal or added degree in all libraries and repositories and points out that successful reference service blends knowledgeability, insights, and an ability to listen, to question, to analyze and to learn.

The Paper Chase: Reference Service in the Bank's Archives

Anne Van Camp

The Chase Manhattan Bank is a global institution which provides a wide range of financial and related services to customers throughout the world. More than 300 branches, over 50 major subsidiaries, 6,000 correspondent banks and 40,000 employees make Chase the third largest bank in the United States.

The Chase today is the product of a long, complicated and interesting history which reflects the social, political and economic development of New York, the United States and the world.

HISTORICAL BACKGROUND

The earliest antecedent of Chase Manhattan was the Bank of The Manhattan Company founded in 1799. The Manhattan Company was originally formed as a water company for the City of New York. The utility company was intended to provide pure water for the city in an effort to combat a yellow fever epidemic. The group of founders, all leading citizens of New York, included in their number Alexander Hamilton and Aaron Burr.

The Bank came into existence with a clause added to the original charter of the company stating that surplus capital from the water company could be used in a banking function. Over the years, this clause was the subject of a great deal of political contention especially among the founding members. Nevertheless, the banking activity of the company proved far more lucrative and successful than did the waterworks, which were sold to the city in 1840.

The Chase National Bank, the other major antecedent of Chase

The author is Second Vice President and Archivist, Chase Manhattan Bank, N.A., One Chase Manhattan Plaza—23, New York, NY 10081.

© 1986 by The Haworth Press, Inc. All rights reserved.

Manhattan was formed in 1877 by John Thompson. Thompson named the new bank after Salmon P. Chase to express his admiration for the former Secretary of the Treasury.

In 1955 when the Bank of The Manhattan Company and the Chase National Bank merged, each of these institutions brought special areas of strength to the new Chase Manhattan Bank. The Bank of The Manhattan Company had merged with and acquired several small local New York area banks and as a result was a strong domestic retail bank. The Chase National through its own mergers and acquisitions had become a leading corporate, correspondent, and international bank.

The creation of Chase Manhattan enabled the institution to develop along what have been Chase's three strongest lines of business: consumer banking, commercial and institutional banking, and international financial services, including commercial and merchant banking as well as other transactional businesses. In all these areas, Chase has long prided itself as an institution that provides high quality services to its customers.

ORGANIZATION OF THE ARCHIVES

The Chase Manhattan Archives was formally organized in 1975, as a secure central repository where records of Chase having permanent value would be preserved, maintained, and made available for research and reference use. The creation of the archives was the result of a growing realization on the part of senior management that the institution's history is a valuable corporate asset and an important management resource.

The initial years of the program were spent locating, transferring and arranging records in the archives. Fortunately many of the older records documenting the corporate activity of the antecedent banks were still available and housed in the records center. Records of the original water company were also located. Once the initial surveying and appraising were well underway, efforts were turned toward more current activities of the bank and areas of active record solicitation were identified.

Today, 10 years later, the Chase Archives houses nearly 3500 cubic feet of records covering the years 1799 to the present. The collection includes corporate documentation, executive records, policies and procedural guidelines, major business and product information. It is the official repository for copies of all Chase publications and major reports. And the archives holds an extensive photograph collection of approximately 500,000 images.

Major responsibilities of the archives include record appraisal and collection, arrangement and description of archival materials, research and reference service, and outreach. All of these activities are interdependent.

ARRANGEMENT AND DESCRIPTION

Records within the collection are organized in the traditional archival scheme of record groups. The record groups reflect both the organization of the institution and some of the special types of material within the collection such as publications and photographs. Records of each of the major antecedent banks are kept as discrete record groups. Records of other merged banks are also a separate group documenting over sixty different institutions. The largest and most rapidly expanding groups are those that contain records of the Corporation, the bank's departments and divisions, and its current subsidiaries and affiliates.

Within record groups are subgroups, record series and subseries arranged to reflect the manner in which the records were generated or used. For example, within the record group called Chase Manhattan Bank Departments/Divisions, a subgroup would be Corporate Communications-Marketing & Advertising and a record series would be "Marketing Research Reports"; another series might be "Advertising Campaigns."

The level of detail used to describe records within the collection varies significantly. Factors used to evaluate the level of description warranted include importance of the information, level of expected use, original order of the material, and staff time available to process and describe records. The broadest level of description is the accession record. Each group of materials transfered to the archives is given a chronological accession number and a brief record of the collection's provenance, scope and contents is created. Its presence and location are then noted in the appropriate record group listing.

For each accession, a container list is usually prepared, often at the folder title level. This gives greater control over the records and allows for easy access to the information. Container lists are filed in the appropriate record group listings as well. The office of origin receives a copy of this finding aid enabling them to readily identify records they may need to use.

Sometimes, collections require description at a much greater level of detail. If the collection contains a great deal of important information and has a potentially exceptional research value, description may be necessary at a folder contents or even item level. Examples of some Chase collections where this detail has been warranted are the David Rockefeller Papers (former Chairman of Chase), Marketing Research Reports, and the Photograph Collection.

AUTOMATED INFORMATION SYSTEM

To enhance the ability to describe collections at the appropriate level and to locate and retrieve information rapidly, the archives is currently using a WANG VS 100 integrated information system. The system supports both data processing and word processing.

The system is used to produce several kinds of printed guides to the collections. These guides are common forms of finding aids used in archival repositories. Creation of access guides for archival collections can often be a tedious, time-consuming project requiring great attention to detail and frequent revision and updating of information. Using the computer to assist in the generation of finding aids substantially reduces the time involved, improves the accuracy and timeliness of the guides, and allows for a depth of indexing that would not be feasible if done manually.

The computer programs were developed to locate information based on traditional methods of archival access and on anticipated uses of the collections. Information can be located by using a variety of search criteria, including a date or range of dates, a key word, a record type, or any combination thereof. Maintaining collection descriptions on the system enables the processor to correct or update information rapidly. It also allows the user to search through a great deal of information quickly and accurately.

The word processing capabilities of the system are used to handle many of the daily operational needs of the archives, including correspondence, budget maintenance, reports, and some of the simpler forms of collection guides. Larger or more complicated information handling and retreival needs are usually met by data processing functions.

REFERENCE AND OUTREACH SERVICES

Reference service in the Chase archives is one of its most important functions, and is certainly the most time-consuming and the most consequential to those outside the department. At least 50% of all staff time is spent on reference work. The staff currently consists of two full-time professionals and one part-time clerical assistant. An average of 35 requests per week are answered. Nearly 60% of all requests are from within the bank and the remainder come from outside the institution.

Internal requests come from every area of the bank. Offices that have records on deposit in the archives frequently need to have information from their own records. Legal department researchers often need to use past records regarding bank policy, procedures or personnel. Corporate communications staff heavily use past speeches, clippings, photographs and publications. The percentage of internal requests often increases as a result of archives' outreach activities such as an exhibit for employees, a presentation at a large meeting, or an article within an internal publication.

External requests are extremely varied. Users range from photo researchers for textbooks to scholarly researchers. Urban archeologists have used records from the early water company to document the early Manhattan water system. Economic historians have done significant research in several areas of U.S. economic development.

Requests are most frequently received over the telephone or by personal visit, and a modest number of external requests are made by mail. How a research request is completed depends on the nature of the inquiry. If the request is placed in person or over the phone, the archivist must interview the requestor to try to determine specific information requirements. Few researchers know the best approach to an archives. Most requests start out as very general, exploratory questions like "What do you have on the history of the bank?" or "I need to use the records from the International Department," or "Does the archives have any photos of branches?"

The archivist must counter these questions with others like "What particular period of history are you interested in?" or "Are you looking for information on the International Department or on the bank's activity within a particular area or country?" or "Which branch are you looking for?" Continued interviewing might demonstrate the real questions are: "When did the merger take place and how many employees were in the bank at that time?" or "What kind of presence has the bank had in the Middle East over the last 20 years?'' or ''Do you have any interior photographs of the 64th Street & Madison Avenue branch from the 1950s?''

Of course, the process is greatly simplified in this brief description, but the interview method is clearly an important step in meeting the requestor's need efficiently and effectively. It has been proven repeatedly that this will save time and will invariably result in a much more satisfactory response. It will help determine whether a single item of information is needed, whether a group of documents is required, whether staff can execute the research or whether the requestor really does need to come in and do in-depth research using primary documents.

Requests by mail are usually either for single item information or are descriptions of research needs and requests for appointments to visit the archives. Occasionally individuals will request the archives staff to do extensive research on their behalf. Normally these individuals would be informed of what materials are available and would be encouraged to use the archives to conduct their own research.

Using the finding aids available and knowing the general scope of the collection, the archivist can usually locate appropriate material very quickly. Researchers are allowed to use most of the finding aids in the archives but generally need some initial direction in using the most appropriate guides and listings. Once research needs have been determined and appropriate materials identified, access considerations must be examined.

ACCESS POLICIES

Controlling access to information is important in virtually any archives. At Chase access to the archives is regulated by a carefully constructed access policy. Banks are quasi-public institutions in that services they provide and information they handle are highly regulated by governmental agencies and legislation. While some information must be disclosed to the public, other information is required by law to be kept confidential. Aside from information governed by regulation, the corporation also generates information that it is willing to disclose and other information it wishes to protect for competitive or other business reasons.

Without an access policy covering the use of archival material, the archivist is highly vulnerable and must make ad hoc or arbitrary decisions. This situation can result in discriminatory access practices, criticism for being unduly secretive or restrictive, or inadvertent harmful disclosure.

At Chase, the access policy for the archives is specifically outlined in the Corporate Organization and Policy Guide. The policy includes clear descriptions of restrictions, time limits on restrictions, procedures for determining restrictions and a statement outlining lines of administrative authority. It is the responsibility of the archivists to carry out this policy.

Basically, there are three access categories of records in the archives: open, restricted, and closed. Open records are those which may be available to employees as well as persons not affiliated with the company. Included are records originally intended for public use and other material approved for public release. Restricted records are those which, though not open to the public, may be made available to employees for business related research. Closed records are those which, for a specified period of time, are available only to the office of origin and the archives staff. At Chase, records are normally closed for 20 years from the time of their creation. Some records, for example, minutes of the Board of Directors meetings, are closed for much longer periods of time.

If records that are restricted or closed are requested by individuals outside the office of origin, written permission to release the information to the requestor must be obtained from an appropriate official in the originating office.

When it has been determined that a researcher may use records in the archives and the appropriate materials have been located, the researcher must complete an application for use which also outlines the regulations of the department. All materials must be used in the archives under staff supervision and researchers are required to observe copyright laws and must take care not to alter or damage materials being used.

EVALUATION OF REFERENCE SERVICES

Upon completion of research, the archivist may conduct another brief interview with the researcher to determine whether the records were arranged and described adequately, and to determine any research potential of the records previously not apparent to the archivists. This is one way to help evaluate reference service.

For each reference request the archives handles, an inquiry form is completed. Information recorded includes date, name, address and phone number of requestor, type of request (internal or external, in-person, letter or phone), brief description of the nature of inquiry, who handled the request and when it was completed. There is also an indication of how the request was handled, whether information was given over the phone or sent out or whether the request was referred elsewhere. While these statistics are somewhat useful, the value of such reference statistics as a reflection of work load is limited; some reference questions take only minutes to complete while others may take days. On the other hand, such records indicate audience served and types of information needed and used.

Because reference service is a major part of our raison d'etre, virtually *all* requests are completed within 5 business days, and most in much less time. A portion are answered on the spot. Even if the request cannot be answered or is considered to be inappropriate, the requestor will receive a response or a referral from the archives staff.

While the other responsibilities of the archives are important—collecting, appraising, arranging and describing—they are all executed with the goal of ultimate use and reference service in mind. The archival profession is dedicated to preserving and making information available on an equitable basis. At Chase, the archives prides itself on consistently high quality reference service. The result is a strongly supported, useful and heavily used archives.

The Challenge of Contemporary Records: Reference Service in a Labor and Urban Archives

Philip P. Mason

The years since World War II have witnessed a remarkable growth in archives and manuscript depositories in the United States and Canada. The National Archives, which was established in 1934, greatly expanded its activities after the war assuming responsibility for records management, a more active National Historical Publication and Records Commission and the Presidential Library System. The years since 1945 also have seen the development of hundreds of new archival programs, including those representing churches, business firms, professional organizations and other institutions.

The proliferation of archives included the development of programs devoted to a particular subject theme. Although interest in elite groups in American society continued to dominate historical scholarship, increased attention was given to new areas of research. Immigration, women, peace movements, social welfare, labor, urban and industrial America, radical and protest movements, Blacks, Native Americans, and various ethnic groups were among the subjects or themes around which major archival institutions were established. Most of these new programs were associated with colleges and universities in the United States and Canada.

HISTORY FROM THE BOTTOM UP

There were other differences in the new subject-oriented archives compared to archives which existed before 1950. Unfettered by tra-

---

The author is Professor of History and Director of the Archives of Labor History and Urban Affairs, Wayne State University, Detroit, Michigan 48202. He has through the years made significant contributions to archival literature.

© 1986 by The Haworth Press, Inc. All rights reserved.

ditional collecting practices and free from conservative governing boards, the new archival programs collected the records relating to the "history of the inarticulate" and "history from the bottom up." Furthermore, unlike older archival programs which reflected the views of most historians and seldom accepted collections less than a generation old, new archives collected contemporary records as well as papers of persons still active in private and public life.

Another new development in the period since 1950 was the increased size of contemporary archival collections. Up to the 1950s a personal collection consisting of 25,000 items was considered a large collection. Twenty years later it was not uncommon for archivists to accept collections of personal papers of over a million items. The volume of organizational records increased at an even greater rate. The sheer size of archival collections and their contemporary nature created problems for the archivist which were unknown several decades earlier or which had existed on a much more manageable scale. For example, the appraisal of contemporary collections, conservation activities, arrangement and description, legal problems such as libel, confidentiality and literary property rights, access policy, and security were altered as a result. These changes in collecting had an equally profound impact upon the reference services provided by archival institutions. Many archival institutions are still trying to develop reference procedures and policies to cope with contemporary collections.

ARCHIVES OF LABOR AND URBAN AFFAIRS

The Archives of Labor and Urban Affairs at Wayne State University in Detroit is typical of the subject or theme oriented archival institutions established in the last three decades. It provides a case study of how reference services develop in such an institution and the problems that face archivists who deal primarily with contemporary records.[1]

The Archives at Wayne State University was established in 1960 to collect and preserve the records of the American labor movement, with special emphasis upon industrial unionism and related social, economic and political reform movements in the United States. A second broad theme is workers, working conditions and the nature of work. Later, the theme of urban affairs was added to the collecting scope, although until the present time it has been largely limited to urban developments in the greater Detroit and Southeastern Michigan region. The majority of the collections relate to the period after 1920, though there are some significant materials that date back to the early 20th century.[2]

The Archives is the official depository for eight major international unions: The United Automobile, Aerospace and Agricultural Implement Workers of America (UAW), the Industrial Workers of the World (IWW), The Newspaper Guild (TNG), the American Federation of Teachers (AFT), the American Federation of State, County and Municipal Employees (AFSCME), the Air Line Pilots Association (ALPA), the Association of Flight Attendants (AFA), and the United Farm Workers of America (UFW). Files of the Congress of Industrial Organizations (CIO), covering the years 1935-1955, are also held in the Archives. In addition to the inactive files of the international union, the Archives collects the files of regional, state and local subdivisions, including the records of dissident worker movements, such as Miners for Democracy, Dodge Revolutionary Union Movement (DRUM), Steel Workers Fight Back, and the Association for Union Democracy.

The papers of numerous reform organizations that have assisted the labor movement have been collected by the Archives, including the Workers Defense League, the Association of Catholic Trade Unionists, the National Farm Workers Ministry, National Sharecroppers Fund, the Peoples Song Library, Center for Community Change, Committee for National Health Insurance, Citizens Crusade Against Poverty, the Coalition of Labor Union Women, the Urban Environmental Conference, Inc., and News and Letters.

The personal files or papers of labor union leaders at the national, regional and local level, rank and file union members, labor journalists, church leaders, public officials, reformers, community leaders and others associated with various reform movements are also collected. Special attention has been given to the papers of individuals who have been active in those organizations which have placed their inactive files in the Archives. Thus, in order to supplement union files, the Archives has acquired the personal files of the Reuther brothers—Walter, Victor and Roy; Cesar Chavez; Jerry Wurf; Leonard Woodcock; Douglas Fraser; Clarence Sayen, and other labor leaders.

The files of women active in labor and reform movements have also been a high priority on the Archives' collection list. Among the collections given to the Archives are the papers of Mary Heaton

Vorse, Katherine Pollack Ellickson, Mary White Ovington, Phyllis Collier, Edith Christenson, Jean Gould, Lillian Hatcher, Dorothy Haener, Mildred Jeffrey, Delores Huerta, Mary Herrick, Selma Borchardt, Mary Van Kleeck, Olga Madar, Loretta Moore, Matilda Robbins, Carrie Overton, Mary Wheeler and Raya Dunayevskaya.

In addition to the written record, the Labor Archives, from its establishment, has utilized oral history to supplement its holdings. For the most part, oral history interviews have been related directly to the collecting themes of the Archives. For example, more than 175 interviews relate directly to the founding and early development of the UAW and AFSCME, two of the major archival holdings. Oral history has been used also to enrich the Archives' holdings on various individuals who have given their personal papers to the Archives, as well as to obtain information on such subject areas as the role of Blacks, other minorities, and women in the labor movement.

The audio-visual section of the Labor Archives contains extensive source material on labor and the other themes of the program. Nearly one million photographs and films have been collected from a variety of sources: unions, union members, personal donors, newspapers and commercial photographers. They document important strikes and other events, work scenes, conventions, meetings, parades, Labor Day and other celebrations as well as the lives and careers of individuals. Among the IWW-related collections, for example, are unique photographs of the funerals of Joe Hill, Frank Little and other union martyrs, the Everett Massacre, the deportation of "Wobblies" from Bisbee, and the violent Wheatland, Patterson and Lawrence strikes. A more recent acquisition received in 1983 was 140 photographs of the noted labor photographer, Lewis Hine.

Other pictorial representations of history give whimsical, esthetic and dramatic views of historical events. For example, broadsides, posters, bulletins, cartoons, murals and paintings, and similar illustrations form another important segment of the audio-visual collection. Among the recent acquisitions of the collection are four postcards written by Joe Hill shortly before he was executed by the state of Utah in 1915. What makes these postcards unique is that on each one he drew a cartoon. The last one is in color and depicts a Christmas celebration.[3]

The film collection is another rich, albeit untapped, resource of the Archives. In addition to the films produced about the labor movement, the Archives has acquired several thousand films—most of which are raw footage—depicting strikes, conventions and similar meetings, parades, work scenes and related events. For example, films given to the archives by a major Detroit television station provide on-the-spot news coverage of many incidents and scenes, which are directly related to Archives' other holdings in the fields of work and social change.

After twenty-five years of operation, the Archives at Wayne State University has become one of the nation's leading depositories for labor and related material. It contains about 95 million items or about 50,000 linear feet of records, 850,000 photographs, broadsides, and posters; 20,000 films, tape recordings, and related audiovisual material; and a reference library of 20,000 volumes. The Archives is housed in the Walter P. Reuther Libary, a facility given to the University by the United Automobile Workers, on the main campus of Wayne State University.

There has been a steady increase in the use of the Archives by researchers, especially since 1975 when the Reuther Library building was completed. The building itself has given the facility visibility on campus and in the greater Detroit community. More important in publicizing the resources of the Reuther Library have been the increasing number of publications—dissertations, monographs, journal articles and books—which have cited the Archives. Although reference service has always been a major part of the archival program at Wayne State University, it has taken on greater importance because of the growing number of researchers, new trends in the study of labor history, and the imaginative way in which photographs, films and oral history have been used for the study of the past.

FACTORS AFFECTING REFERENCE

Reference procedures and policies in the Archives of Labor and Urban Affairs are determined by a number of factors, including the manner in which collections are acquired, terms of access, arrangement and description of collections, users and areas of research, reference analyses and legal problems.

With the exception of a few collections obtained from dealers, and, of course, published materials and reference books, all of the archival material is acquired through gift or loan arrangements. As a matter of policy, the Archives of Labor and Urban Affairs does not accept records of an on-going labor or other membership organization, as an outright gift. It does accept such collections on loan or deposit under specific terms of agreement, covering such areas as access, literary property rights, retrieval, and the responsibility of the Archives to process and preserve collections. The Archives' staff negotiates access terms with each donor. The UAW, for example, has agreed to make available to researchers all of their inactive files transferred to the Archives that are more than ten years old; those files less than ten years old are closed except with specific permission of the union. All published material, such as proceedings, newspapers, journals, pamphlets, contracts, etc., are available without restriction. Other unions and organizations have adopted similar access provisions ranging from 15 years closure to no restrictions. Some unions have provided that union members may have access to all of their union's records regardless of age.

This "loan" arrangement has not been widely adopted by other archives, most of whom insist that only an outright gift is acceptable. At Wayne State University the loan or deposit agreement has worked very effectively and has allowed the Archives to obtain collections of valuable records which otherwise would not have been available. Furthermore, the arrangement has been beneficial to the University and the Archives in other ways. In legal actions, such as the issuance of a subpoena to examine documents in a collection, the Archives has taken the position that it is not a party to the action because it does not own the records; it is up to the international union or the organization which owns the records to respond to such legal action. Terms of the loan arrangement also puts the Archives on notice that it must inventory and process a collection promptly and that the collection must be made available to researchers in a reasonable period of time.

The Archives' staff assists other donors in establishing terms of access and in identifying those groups of records or single items which should be closed for a longer period of time or removed from the collection entirely. This policy is based upon our experience in dealing with archival collections, especially large contemporary ones, whose sheer bulk often hides the location of sensitive, highly personal items. We have discovered also that even in smaller collections, donors are usually unaware of the total content of a collection or the confidential items that have been placed there. For example, the Archives has discovered such items as personal income tax statements, investigator's reports relating to pending divorce proceedings, medical and psychiatric records, etc., that have been placed in a file and forgotten. On occasion, a donor will destroy such sensitive items, but for the most part those having historical value have been preserved, even though it is necessary to restrict access to them for a specified period of time.

ACCESS WITH REASONABLE RESTRICTIONS

Some researchers have been critical of restrictions upon access to records in the Archives, maintaining that a public institution such as Wayne State University should allow unlimited access to all records in its custody, and indeed, that the Archives should not accept any collections which have such restrictions.[4] This criticism represents a naiveté that does not emanate from archival experience. Unless an archives is willing to accept collections with *reasonable* restrictions upon access, they will remain in the custody of the donor often in unsuitable and unsafe storage conditions, unavailable for research. Furthermore, one could take the position that international unions, like the UAW, are extremely liberal in their ten-year access rule. One need only examine the restrictive policies of the automotive companies, for example, to see how enlightened is the policy of the UAW.

The difficult problem facing reference archivists is how to apprise researchers that a part of a collection in which they are interested has been closed or restricted and concomitantly how to notify interested researchers that sections of a collection have been opened since their last visit. The Archives' policy is to give as much information to reseachers about closed collections as possible as long as such information does not violate the wishes of a donor. Researchers are also advised of a blanket closure, such as the 10-year rule relating to the UAW and AFSCME records.

Another issue relates to access by researchers to unprocessed collections. As a matter of policy, most archives are reluctant to allow users access to such collections even though they are relevant to their research. The reasons are obvious. For example, at Wayne State University, we have an agreement with most donors that the Archives' staff will carefully examine each collection to determine if any papers are included by mistake that the donor wishes to remain private. Furthermore, until a collection has been arranged and described according to archival procedures, it is usually difficult for a researcher to cite the location of a particular document. In a few cases, however, this policy is waived so that a researcher, under publication deadline, for example, may examine an unprocessed collection. More often, however, the Archives will arrange to process such collections immediately if there is an urgent need by researchers.

Regardless of the fairness of this policy towards closed or unprocessed collections, there have been abuses. Some researchers become angry if they discover that a collection in which they have an interest is closed or unprocessed and demand that it be made available to them. The Reference Reading Room as well as the Director's office have been the scene of serious and even noisy confrontations when this situation arises. On several occasions, determined researchers have pressured or attempted to persuade members to divulge information about the content of closed or unprocessed collections.

SCREENING USERS

Another area involving reference work in an archives relates to the policy of screening users of the archival collections. At most public archives there are no restrictions as long as a researcher does not mishandle archival material. At Wayne State University it was found necessary to be more restrictive and place some restraints upon the groups of researchers who could use the Archives. International union and community groups were willing to make their inactive historical files available to persons doing serious research, but not to police agencies or "union busting" organizations. If such restrictions were not placed upon their collections, they refused to place them in the Archives. As a result of this situation, and in order to encourage the preservation of important historical files, the Wayne State University Board of Governors adopted the policy that users of the Archives should be engaged in "serious or scholarly research." The Director of the Archives was given the responsibility of interpreting this definition.

Up to now there have been few problems in enforcing this rule. High school students, rank and file unionists, and genealogists are given free access to holdings, along with graduate students, faculty members and other scholars. The political, religious or other biases of researchers are never considered. Indeed as long as a collection is used properly without willful damage, there are few restraints.

The only specific group that is not allowed to examine archival holdings, except, of course, those records, such as newspapers, journals and other publications already in the public domain, are officers of federal, state and local police agencies. As a matter of policy, members of the University's Public Safety staff are not allowed to use the archival collections nor are they allowed access in those parts of the Reuther Library where archival collections are stored. Moreover, investigative reporters searching indiscriminately for a sensational story are not encouraged to use the Archives. Nor are the legal or public relations staff of the automotive companies who want to examine the files of the UAW. Nevertheless, such requests are made periodically by the auto companies, especially before each round of major contract negotiations. The staff of National Right to Work Organization and other groups whose objectives are to destroy unions are denied access to union collections, unless they have specific permission from donors.

Despite these rules, there have been attempts to bypass or circumvent them. On occasion, users have given false information about their research interest. Indeed, on one occasion, an officer in a federal intelligence agency enrolled in an economics course at Wayne State University in order to gain access to a specific collection. It was not a study of historical subject or labor economics that he was interested in; rather, it was personal data on several union members.

THEFT AND MUTILATION: A CONTINUING PROBLEM

Another related problem which has been of deep concern to the Labor Archives relates to theft and mutilation of archival materials. Wayne State University is not alone in dealing with this problem. Archives and libraries in the United States and Canada have been the victims of thieves in increasing numbers in the last 30 years. Thousands of valuable archival records have been stolen, some for their autograph or resale value and others because a thief wants to possess the letters of a particular individual. Another problem relates to the defacement or mutilation of documents. The motives for such behavior vary. For example, in order to qualify for membership in a patriotic or other organization, a user may want to prove that an ancestor came to the United States or Canada during a certain period so he or she removes a document from the collection or in some cases alters the document.

Another equally serious violation involves the defacing, mutilation, or even theft of a document because a researcher does not agree with the contents, or because it may challenge the researcher's own scholarship. On one occasion, a researcher cut out a section of a document which purported to show that Walter P. Reuther was actually a member of the Communist Party during the 1930s. The motive for this defacement was that she "did not want Reuther to get credit for anything the Communists had accomplished." It is relatively simple for a user to identify autograph items of substantial market value, but it is almost an impossible task for an institution to protect such documents against defacement.

As a result of theft, defacement and attempts of unauthorized persons to gain access to archival collections, a comprehensive security program has been developed at the Reuther Library. Special alarm systems are installed on all outer perimeter doors. All keys and locks are periodically changed and janitorial work must be completed during regular working hours.

In addition, there are special security procedures for the Reading Room. All researchers must check their coats, briefcases, purses and other similar items in lockers, provided free of charge, outside the Reading Room. Upon registration a researcher is assigned a specified space at a reading table where boxes of records are brought for examination and note paper is provided. Furthermore, periodic checks are made of all collections that are used by researchers. A professional archivist is on duty at all times and closed-circuit television monitors the Reading Room. The records maintained allow the staff to determine the names of researchers on any given day, the table assignment of each, collection and box numbers used, and items copied. This data has proved invaluable in tracing any missing items.

Other individual measures are utilized to insure security. Each researcher is required to provide positive identification, and to complete a detailed application which cites information on institutional affiliation, permanent and local address, nature of research, and permission to publicize the research topic in the Archives' Newsletter. References are requested and frequently checked also. Moreover, researchers are informed that the Reading Room is monitored by closed circuit television.

In 1975, when the Reuther Library building was opened, users frequently voiced criticism about the rules relating to the use of the Reading Room, especially the provision for closed circuit television. The charge of "Big Brother is watching," was heard often. But today there is little opposition to such rules. The Archives' staff answers any question about our security and Reading Room procedures and explains the rationale for these policies. The choice is with researchers; if they object they do not have to use the Archives.

GUIDES TO THE COLLECTIONS

The Archives provides a series of finding aids for the researcher. *A Guide to the Archives*, describing all of the Reuther Library holdings, was published in 1974 and will be revised and updated soon.[5] Plans are underway also to publish guides to collections relating to a particular subject or theme such as labor and politics, reform movements, ethnic minorities, labor and the theatre, Blacks and Civil Rights, and women in labor and reform movements. Furthermore, the Archives' *Newsletter* includes information on recent acquisitions and newly-processed collections.

The Archives uses the standard Guide to describe individual collections which are arranged and described according to the archival principles of provenance and sanctity of the original order. Each guide contains detailed background data on the organization, family or individual involved. The size of the collection, the years covered and a list of key correspondents and subjects are also included. The Archives' collections are arranged and described by record series, usually to the folder level. A useful aid is the index at the end of each Guide which facilitates retrieval of material in the collection. In addition, the Archives will have computer facilities within the year to supplement existing word processing capabilities.

Standardization of the Guides is achieved by staff training sessions, and a comprehensive processing manual. A senior staff member has the responsibility of approving all Guides as well as the supervision of all graduate archival students.

Despite the high quality of the Guides, the Archives recognizes the limited usefulness of such tools. The sheer size and volume of many contemporary collections makes it impossible to identify every key correspondent or important topic or subject. Furthermore, archivists who process collections must be able to project future research trends as well as to be knowledgeable about current ones. In order to constantly update Guides, the Archives has established a model program to periodically review and re-describe collections reflecting new research trends and interests.

In addition to the Guides, researchers are put in contact with staff members who have expertise in a special subject area or knowledge of particular collections. For example, certain archival staff members are particularly informed about one or two of the major collections in the Archives, such as the UAW, the United Farm Workers, AFSCME, AFT, the Air Line Pilots Association and the Industrial Workers of the World. Arrangements are made for researchers to meet these staff specialists and to receive individualized assistance.

Nevertheless, like most archives, the Reuther Library relies heavily upon the subject knowledge of the researcher in using archival collections. The user is usually more familiar with the topic than the archivist staff and is able to see relationships and recognize valuable data. In this way, the archival staff can better understand the significance of a particular collection even more by contact and feedback from researchers and also by reading the published monographs or books based upon archival holdings.[6]

AUDIO-VISUAL MATERIALS

The Archives' audio-visual collection has received widespread attention from researchers, although the reference procedures differ significantly from those of traditional archival holdings. The film and photograph collections illustrate the archival holdings at the Reuther Library. In fact, the subject categories in the audio-visual collection closely correlate with the persons and events relating to labor in America in the manuscript collections of the Archives. Occasionally a researcher looks for a photograph of a relative or searches for photographs to hang in a building or office. But in most cases these collections are used by researchers primarily to locate suitable illustrations for their books, or in some cases, for pictorial histories.

The most widespread use of the audio-visual collections is made by producers of films, documentaries and television news programs. In fact, during the past five years more than one hundred major film producers have utilized the pictorial and film holdings of the Labor Archives. For example, much of the background research on the film "Reds" was done at the Labor Archives, utilizing the audio-visual collections as well as archival material and oral history tapes and transcripts. Regretably, historians and other scholars have not yet recognized or utilized the research value of photographs and films as historical records.

Reference service for the film collections differs from traditional archival holdings. Because of the need for special handling of single photographic copies, the Archives uses mylar encapsulation for protection. Film researchers often need to preview hours of raw footage before finding suitable frames for copying. Similarly, users of photographs often want to look at hundreds and even thousands of images before making a selection. This reference activity usually requires constant individualized assistance by the Archives' staff. Such special attention also justifies a user fee for photographs and films needed for commercial or profit-making ventures.

The Archives staff of the Reuther Library also provides reference services to donors. Frequently, for example, international unions that have placed their inactive files in the Archives need to retrieve particular documents or locate relevant information about a particular subject. The Air Line Pilots Association, for example, has often requested data on accidents involving a particular type of aircraft. Legal case files are also requested often, usually with a plea that they are needed urgently. The United Farm Workers requested recently the names and addresses of all volunteers and full-time staff who worked on the Grape Boycott in the early 1970s. Our policy is to assist donors whenever possible in order to justify the deposit of their inactive files in the Reuther Library.

A more difficult problem relates to the increasing number of mail and phone requests from researchers who want information on individual documents or groups of records. Although the Archives' staff attempts to provide this type of reference service—for example, sending copies of Guides to researchers—there are times when such requests require extra work for the staff. Phone inquiries are often even more time consuming and difficult, and are increasing because of special phone services available to researchers.

YOUNGER SCHOLARS—HOW WELL PREPARED?

Another related problem which has led to a noticeable increase in the demand for archival reference services over the past 25 years has been the lack of training of graduate students and other younger scholars in the use of archival material. It is evident, for example, that we can no longer assume that history or other graduate students have received solid training in bibliography or the use of archival reference guides as tools, or the critical use of archival materials. Researchers often arrive at the Reuther Library without being aware of the collections available here or at other institutions. On one occasion, for example, a graduate student from a Washington, D.C. area university, arrived at Wayne State for a study of the NAACP—without realizing that the official files of that organization are in the Library of Congress Manuscript Division. He made the long and costly trip to Detroit to find out this information.

As a result of this situation, the Reuther archival reference staff has been required to spend an increasing amount of time in assisting researchers at the beginning stages of their research. Also, to help such archives users, the Reuther Library has acquired extensive guides, inventories and finding aids published by other archival institutions, especially those covering labor or related collections. Many patrons are unfamiliar with regulations relating to literary property or statutory copyright provisions. As a result, the Archives' staff is constantly apprising users of such provisions and the need to secure permission to quote documents for which the Reuther Library does not own the copyright.

REFERENCE SERVICE: SIGNIFICANT CHANGES

Reference service in the Reuther Library has changed significantly during the past 25 years. Approximately 1,300 researchers visit the Archives each year, spending about one week on the average. Some patrons, of course, spend weeks and even months at the Archives. Beginning in 1985 and continuing for three academic years, the Archives will host two Rockefeller Foundation Residency scholars each year. In addition, the Archives receives hundreds of phone calls and written inquiries, many of which lead to user visits to the Archives.

Statistics are kept on the nature of the research, subjects or topics, amount of time spent, collections used and publications based upon such research. This information is used for a variety of purposes. We can predict the use of the Reading Room, chart peak loads, determine the frequency of use of particular collections and identify security problems. The nature of the research also assists the archival staff in establishing collecting priorities, appraisal, conservation and restoration needs, and in determining the order in which collections are processed. Every archival staff member of the Reuther Library, regardless of archival specialty, is assigned duty at the reference desk. This assignment broadens the perspective of the staff and contributes significantly to an understanding of the total archival process.

The changing nature of Archives in the United States and Canada in the last twenty-five years has brought about significant changes in all aspects of archival work. Except for the process of evaluation or appraisal, no area has been more profoundly affected than reference services. More and more, the reputation of our archival institution is based upon how effectively such services are presented to the research public. Archivists must continue to give reference service major attention.

NOTES

1. Philip P. Mason. "The Archives of Labor and Urban Affairs, Walter P. Reuther Library, Wayne State University". *Labor History* 23(Fall 1982): 485-581.

2. "Labor Archives in the United States". *Archivum* 27(1980): 160-183.

3. Joe Hill. "Cartoonist". *Labor History* 25(Fall 1984): 553-557.

4. Alonzo L. Hamby and Edward Weldon. *Access to the Papers of Recent Public Figures: The New Harmony Conference*. Bloomington, Ind.: Organization of American Historians, 1977.

5. Warner Pflug. *A Guide to the Archives of Labor History and Urban Affairs*. Detroit: Wayne State University Press, 1974.

6. Mary Jo Pugh. "The Illusion of Omniscience: Subject Access and the Reference Archivist". In *A Modern Archives' Reader*. National Archives and Records Service, 1984.

The Manuscript Repository That Isn't

Charles Clement

INTRODUCTION

When manuscripts with intrinsic relationships are gathered into one place, that place is generally known as a manuscript repository. Such places are not archives per se, and they're not libraries.

What, then, is an institution that is manuscript research-oriented but is not a repository of actual manuscripts? One with an ad-hoc collection of copied portions of manuscript collections that have no intrinsic rationale for being together based on any connection to their original purpose as records? A collection of hundreds of thousands of such manuscript copies, together with all that it would take to make them usable (reference books, catalogs, staff, etc.), would constitute an oddity in the information world. Such an oddity exists in Salt Lake City, Utah, and is called the Genealogical Library of The Church of Jesus Christ of Latter-Day Saints.

The Genealogical Library cannot really be called a "manuscript repository" because the manuscripts are still "reposited" elsewhere. It cannot be called an archive in nearly any recognized sense of the word. The manuscript copies are not even on paper—they are on film. The "records" in its extensive collection were not created to ever be brought together by any rationale. But they *have* been brought together and that which has caused it is a frenetic phenomenon known as "genealogy"; i.e., the search for family connections by individuals. Because it supports genealogical research with open stacks free to the public and uses somewhat standard library cataloging for bibliographic control, it is called a "library." But the truly international collection, which is almost exclusively manuscripts on film accessed via somewhat standard cataloging, suggests the uniqueness of the "library" and its reference functions.

The author is Manager of Technical Services at the LDS Genealogical Library in Salt Lake City, Utah 84150.

© 1986 by The Haworth Press, Inc. All rights reserved.

REFERENCE SERVICE

One of the major objectives of the Genealogical Library is to *make manuscript records*, handwritten long ago in a foreign language and/or unfamiliar script, *usable by the general public*. This objective includes the provision of individual assistance in the performance of genealogical research, whether in person or by outreach. This requires mainly: (1) effective bibliographic organization, (2) informed, skilled, and helpful reference consultants, and (3) elaborate yet functional reference aids.

(1) As mentioned, somewhat standard practices are followed in bibliographic organization. Books are arranged on shelves in Dewey Decimal sequences that reflect modifications made to enhance genealogical research. Microfilms are numbered by accession within broad categories of numbers blocked out in advance corresponding to broad geographic areas. This eliminates shifting the microfilm collections, otherwise an enormous, laborious, and expensive undertaking.

The library catalog and other finding aids made by the reference staff tend to give very detailed descriptions of books and manuscripts in the collection. Not only does this facet of bibliographic organization help the researcher decide if a given item is pertinent to his research, but it helps to get the very specific parts that will be useful. General descriptions would make all researchers have to search through whole records looking for specific useful parts. Superimposed is the fact that most of the manuscript records are in unfamiliar script and, if one is very far back in his research, in foreign languages as well.

Most cataloging done in the library is original cataloging because the manuscripts and many of the books are not described by anyone else. Most of the 50 catalogers have master's degrees; some have double master's, and many have multiple language skills. Many spend some cross-training time at the reference counters and many are accredited genealogists or have experience doing genealogical research.

Catalogers do their descriptive, classification, and subject work online. Their system configuration consists of two DEC VAX 11/750s (for online application programs) connected via HYPERchannel to an IBM 3081 (for batch programs and data management). This is a progressive arrangement that seems to be working very well.

(2) Reference consultants, skilled in research and personal assistance, greet researchers in reference areas which are organized geographically. Most of the approximately 50 reference consultants have master's degrees and/or are accredited genealogists. Correspondence with researchers is carried on via the most up-to-date WANG word processing system.

(3) Many elaborate reference aids have been designed and compiled manually by staff members over many years. Others have been purchased. A complete and annotated bibliography of the library's reference tools will soon be published. It will contain approximately 300 titles. The following list points out a few of the major *types* of reference tools used at the Genealogical Library. Some of them are:

- Atlases
- Maps
- Gazetteers
- Indexes
- Library catalogs
- Special registers (such as to U.S. censuses, passenger lists, etc.)
- Major source papers
- Big city parish and civil jurisdiction locators
- Handwriting aids for old scripts (paleography)
- Directories
- Family histories
- Local histories
- General histories
- Compiled pedigree files
- Research methodologies

ACCESS

The library's collections and its catalog are arranged geographically except for family histories. Those are alphabetically arranged by surname. Source records and reference works about a country and its parts can be found in the catalog by place-name. Materials by or about certain people or about families can be found in the catalog by surname. So the *access keys* are *place-name* and *surname*. Finding specific things within those categories is a function of the specific research objective, i.e., specific information about birth, marriage, death, immigration, citizenship, migration, and so forth. But some kinds of sources were completed at a state level, some at a county level, and some at a town level. *Before* going to the catalog it pays to consult a couple of reference aids for the country of interest: a gazetteer for exact place-name and a major source paper for level of jurisdiction and type of record needed. After finding the desired place-name in the catalog, item descriptions appear for searching in alphabetical order by type of item (atlases, biographies, census, directories, and so on). This general approach is the same whether searching the catalog online, using the computer-produced microfiche catalog, or the card catalog.

At the present time, searching the catalog online is a privilege of staff only. They use it for bib-checking, for work on special reference tools, for assisting patrons who may be having trouble or whom they may just be assisting with a normal research problem. The same information is available for patron look-up on a microfiche catalog produced by the computer. The advent of microfiche made it possible to put copies of the catalog in all reference areas and behind the reference counters. The computer as a cataloging device made it possible to provide much more detail in each entry in a more readable and sensible format than on cards. A long description on many cards hooked to a drawer-rod is harder to deal with than a nicely formatted image of that description on a single page displayed on a screen. Not only can the researcher read it easily, but he can readily see previous and subsequent headings.

AUTOMATION AND REFERENCE

Our automated cataloging system still does not directly benefit the reference staff very much or the process they use in giving reference service. The reason is that the computer cataloging system merely enabled the card catalog to be replaced by the COM catalog. If anything, it has complicated the reference process while we have been engaged in conversion of one catalog to the other. Having two types of catalogs to train new people in while dealing with psychological attachments by experienced patrons to the "old and familiar" form presents difficulties. These difficulties will end soon and the Computer Output Microfilm (COM) Catalog will have to stand on its own because conversion of the card catalog will be finished by the end of 1986. Could that mean stability?

Automation is insatiable and will not stand still for status-quo. It would be nice to settle down when card catalog conversion is finished and really put the COM Catalog to work. However, the COM Catalog is already dubbed as "interim," a way to give patrons the use of our better cataloging while we work on their "ultimate" finding aid, an OPAC (Online Public Access Catalog)! OPAC prototypes, seeking experience and input from library staff and patrons, will appear even before the last card dies, creating a dual catalog situation once again!

At this point there are three important things to consider: (1) we have been discussing only our main library reference service, (2) the evolution from computerized cataloging tools into true computer-supported reference services is more of a "process" than an "event," and (3) computer-supported reference services involve more things than just automating the catalog.

(1) The Genealogical Library in Salt Lake City has over 500 small, volunteer-staffed branch libraries around the world to whom microfilm is circulated (unless a donor archivist has asked us not to). Reference service in those branch libraries is largely dependent on the quality of the catalog and other reference aids we provide for them, as well as the speed and accuracy of their access to the source records via film circulation. The reason for having these libraries is two-fold: (1) it is a long way to Salt Lake City, and (2) restrictions exist on the circulation of some of our material (requested by repositories where the material was filmed). Because of restrictions, cost of circulating, and because we feel a primary responsibility to our own members, we do not lend our films and books outside our library system. Even so, we do make the main library and branch libraries available to the public. In addition, we answer correspondence from researchers as best we can.

(2) By the time our automated cataloging system has fully evolved to an online reference and research guidance system, we will probably be electronically networked or linked via disk technology to all our branches. In the meantime, the ability to put improved cataloging descriptions on microfiche and distribute them to our branches once a year is a leap forward for our research patrons. This is where the COM Catalog will continue to play a role. Though we're developing an OPAC for the main library, we will be providing COM Catalogs to the branches for some time.

(3) Although little has been computer produced in the library by way of reference materials or services other than the catalog, many

reference consultants are actively engaged in projects to do just that. Making indexes (using volunteer inputters) and developing a "reference data base" of many special access and informational works produced over the years are but a couple of those projects. Also, a number of very useful computer-produced reference tools are purchased from others, such as the tremendous U.S. Census Indexes produced by Accelerated Indexing Systems, Inc. There is yet another index of major consequence to genealogical research. It is not produced by the library reference staff but by the library's parent institution, The Church of Jesus Christ of Latter-Day Saints. The index is called the *International Genealogical Index* (IGI) and contains some 88 million names compiled and submitted by researchers.

The IGI gives parental information as well as individual data and it refers back to sources originally used by the researcher. For more information on why The Church of Jesus Christ of Latter-Day Saints is so involved in genealogical work, please refer to an article in *Library Trends* (Summer, 1983) by David M. Mayfield.

SUMMARY

Integrating automation into reference service is a long process. For us, moving from step 1, an automated cataloging system to step "X", an online reference system linked to all our branches, will have spanned many years. During this time span, the reference environment will have had some unsettling characteristics. It will have seemed uncoordinated at times to both staff and patrons. It is only realistic to admit it so that as we or other organizations navigate our way through the process, we can get the most out of the situation. Singular benefits to be gained along the way can otherwise be overshadowed by "feelings" about the overall development environment in the minds of staff and patrons. Saying right up front that achieving the objective of some form of automated reference service is going to be a fairly long and jittery process may make people feel more secure. When people know they are in a swamp together, they can help each other seek the firm ground along the way, and may even enjoy doing it. Development efforts can be fun, exciting, interesting, and motivational if staff (and even patrons) are properly involved throughout the process.

The Genealogical Library attempts through its collections, its reference aids, and its reference service to make it possible for everyone to have a successful experience delving into the substance of their family history. Automation in cataloging, and further evolution of automated reference services, has enhanced, and will continue to enhance, the possibilities for that success.

A Well-Kept Secret: The Religious Archive as Reference Resource

Rosalie McQuaide

Let it be recorded that in the year 1985, at a time of unprecedented information generation and computerized information access, one of the best-kept secrets of information management—without intending to be—concerns the religious archive as reference resource. Several factors no doubt contribute to the near anonymity of the archives of most religious organizations: the lack of research tools available to the interested researcher, management policies that perhaps place more stress on preservation and conservation than on the creative use of records, and most importantly, a mutual absence of familiarity on the part of the inquirer as to what resources may be found in religious archives and on the part of the archivist as to the nature of current research interests and needs. As part of the larger human problem of the distribution of goods, whether economic, cultural, artistic, recreational, or spiritual, the information gap continues to widen despite the fact that more and more of the precious commodity is being generated and accessed each day. This essay takes a small step toward arresting the imbalance; it describes religious archives in general and the archives of women religious in particular, with respect to their reference resources, and illustrates those resources by drawing upon the documents of one religious organization, the Sisters of St. Joseph of Peace, in reference to two specific areas of historical research: women's issues and the changing perception of women religious.

The religious archive serves as repository for the administrative records, historical documents, and collected memorabilia of the religious organization—church, religious order, or religious society—that generated the records. Some religious archives add

---

The author is Congregational Archivist, Sisters of St. Joseph of Peace, 78 Grand Street, Jersey City, New Jersey 07302.

© 1986 by The Haworth Press, Inc. All rights reserved.

collections to their own corpus of records, enlarging their holdings with valuable historical material that relates in some way to the goals and purposes of the institution they serve. Other religious archives strive simply to maintain their records and to keep up with the accumulation of documentation in the organization.

HISTORICAL BACKGROUND

The archives of women religious within the Catholic Church by and large follow the latter policy. Their holdings consist almost totally of records generated directly by the organization. By many standards, these archives are small. But because the maintenance of archival records by religious organizations has long been mandated by the church, these small collections are distinguished for their continuity, accuracy, and thoroughness. Even beyond mandate, however, the church has encouraged and promoted the archival profession in its task of organizing and preserving vital historical documents and records. In 1881, Pope Leo XIII opened the Vatican Archives to researchers; two years later, he established the Commission for Historical Studies. In 1954 Pope Pius XII constituted the Pontifical Committee of Historical Sciences to ensure the participation of the Holy See in the international pursuit of historical studies. When the International Congress of Historical Sciences held its tenth meeting at the Vatican in 1955, Pius XII addressed the participants. He outlined the position of the church with regard to history and the work of historians:

> The Catholic Church is herself an historical fact; like a powerful chain of mountains, she crosses the history of the past 2,000 years. . . . She believes that she can expect the historian to be informed of the historical awareness she has of herself, that is to say, of the way she considers herself an historical fact and considers her relationship to human history. (*L'Osservatore Romano*, weekly ed. [Dec. 1982])

At that time, the Vatican announced an enlargement of the consultation of the Vatican Archives.

The present Holy Father spoke to the Pontifical Committee in December of 1982, urging the members to "make known to the Holy See the advances in the field of historical studies which directly concern it, and what the suitable paths are, so that it can concretely demonstrate its openmindedness to every legitimate request . . ." (*L'Osservatore Romano*). In our own country, the Catholic Bishops Committee for the Bicentennial published a Document on Ecclesiastical Archives (Nov. 22, 1974) which set forth several goals for the bishops: to inaugurate a nation-wide effort to preserve and organize all existing records and papers; to appoint a properly qualified priest, religious man or woman, or lay person as diocesan archivist; to organize a brief training course conducted by those who have had long experience; and to grant access to the diocesan archives without undue limitations when properly accredited ecclesiastical historians request it.

> In our judgment, no bishop need fear that by opening his archives to scholarly examination, he will expose the Church's past to deliberate attempts at embarrassment. True, scandals and shortcomings may be uncovered, but in these matters we believe that it is still appropriate to follow the admonition of Pope Leo XIII, who in his letter on historical studies, *Saepenumero considerantes*, of August 18, 1883, quoting from Cicero, declared "that the first law of history is not to dare to utter falsehood; the second, not to fear to speak the truth; and, moreover, no room must be left for suspicion of partiality or prejudice."

RELIGIOUS ARCHIVAL TRAINING AND SURVEY

This exhortation of the American Catholic Bishops found a responsive echo among women religious in the U.S. Under the aegis of the Leadership Conference of Women Religious (LCWR), a nation-wide archival project was undertaken during the period 1976-80. Some 375 women religious archivists participated in workshops in basic archival training, and the archival repositories of 569 organizations of women religious—sisters and nuns in the Catholic, Episcopal, and Orthodox churches and deaconesses in the Lutheran, Mennonite, and Methodist churches—were surveyed. This survey led to the publication of *Women Religious History Sources. A Guide to Repositories in the United States (WRHS)* (New York and London: R.R. Bowker, 1983). Edited by Evangeline Thomas, CSJ, with the assistance of Joyce L. White and Lois Wachtel, WRHS can be seen as a companion volume to Andrea Hinding's *Women's History Sources* published by Bowker in 1979. The dedication of the *Guide* signals an awareness on the part of the women religious of the treasures to be found in their archives; even more significantly, however, it signals an openness to research and a genuine interest in sharing these records: "For the research scholar whose use of this guide may lead to a proper evaluation of the role American women religious have played in this nation's religious, social, and cultural history" (WRHS, v.). The *Guide* consists of (1) a list of abbreviations for orders of women, (2) a glossary, (3) the entries for repositories of women religious, which are numbered consecutively and arranged alphabetically by state with alphabetical sublistings by city and name of order, (4) a bibliography, (5) a table of founding dates, (6) a biographical register of foundresses and major superiors, and (7) an index of persons, places, and events; names of foundresses and/or superiors; countries from which foundations were made in the U.S., first and early sites of communities, states in which domestic institutions are (or were) located, and countries in which foreign missions were established; and areas of institutional work, e.g., hospitals and non-institutional work, e.g., ministry among the elderly. *Women Religious History Sources* is a good-sized volume without being unwieldy; its 329 pages are comprehensive but not complicated. It should enjoy an active existence at the elbow of the reference librarian.

SISTERS OF PEACE

A typical entry serves as introduction to the archives of the Sisters of St. Joseph of Peace. The entry reads, in part:

> From the congregation founded by Margaret Anna Cusack in Nottingham, England, in 1884. . . . Founded to create peace in the Church, the world and the family, the congregation ministers in the areas of justice, legislative action, multinational issues, women's equality, and for disarmament and peace in Northern Ireland. Holdings include letters and papers of foundress and major superiors, rules, constitutions and chronicles of the congregation, financial and administrative records . . . formation and retirement records, papers of former and deceased sisters; photographs, scrapbooks, news-

paper articles and a collection of approximately 75 books, most written by the foundress. (WHRS, no.63, p.16)

Like many organizations of women religious, the Sisters of Peace live and minister in widely separated areas; for administrative purposes, the areas are grouped geographically into provinces. This religious organization has three provinces: (1) England, Scotland, Wales, Ireland; (2) Alaska, Oregon, Washington, California; and (3) New York and New Jersey. The general administration of the congregation is conducted by sisters who live and work in the District of Columbia. Sisters working in Africa or in Central America continue membership in the province from which they left for foreign mission work. Each province retains its own administrative records and historical materials, mainly for administrative use. The central or congregational archives is the repository for all general administrative records and for all the holdings listed in WHRS, as given above. Two finding aids for this central archives are available: Catalogue of the Congregational Archives and File Guide. Plans are underway to access the records of the provincial archives by computer, interfiling these records with the congregational records. In this way, researchers can be directed to any archival document of the Sisters of St. Joseph of Peace and copies can be forwarded from any of the four archive locations to the researcher.

INTEREST IN ROOTS

In 1984 the congregation marked its 100th anniversary. This commemoration sparked interest in the work of the order and particularly in the woman who founded the order. Researchers were able to study her letters and her writings in the archives. New sources were discovered in the libraries and archives of Dublin, Rome, and Nottingham. Much more research needs to be done in regard to the life of Margaret Anna Cusack and her spiritual vision and legacy. What, for instance, was her understanding of peace? As will be seen, she herself lives a life that was anything but peaceful in the ordinary sense. How did she relate peace to the struggle for justice? What were her special insights into women's issues? These and other questions remain to be researched; the reference sources are there in the archives for the interested scholar. The reference librarian would want to know also of the sources available in the archives of the Sisters of Peace as they present the history of the Northwest United States. Diaries, newspapers, and correspondence often contain unique accounts of the growth and development of that part of the nation. Fortunately, almost all materials are in good condition and can be photocopied.

To illustrate the value of religious archives as reference resource, particularly in regard to religiously motivated social activism, we draw upon these archives of the Sisters of Peace, whose records are especially strong in two areas of research: women's issues and, related to that, the changed perception of women religious.

A Jersey City newspaper of March 1885 carried an announcement of the opening of a home for working and emigrant girls by the Sisters of Peace, an order founded one year earlier by Mother Mary Francis Clare Cusack, the famous Nun of Kenmare. In the announcement, Mother Clare described the objectives of the Sisters of Peace: (1) to provide houses where emigrant girls shall be taken care of by the sisters at the ports of departure and arrival, (2) to provide homes where friendless girls shall be received until situations are procured for them, (3) to have intelligence offices (what we would now call employment agencies) in these homes where ladies requiring domestic help can apply, (4) to receive girls when out of employment either from ill health or other reasonable causes, (5) to provide homes for those who after a long life of domestic service can no longer undertake active works, either in consequence of the infirmity of old age or from uncurable malady, and (6) to establish institutions for the practical training of girls for domestic services and domestic life. The founding of this order of Peace Sisters in 1884 and the opening of a home for working and emigrant girls in Jersey City in 1885 brought to life a plan of action that had begun to take shape in the mind of Sister Francis Clare twenty years earlier when she departed from her usual practice of writing books of piety and history to address a pressing question of her day, namely, Woman's Work in Modern Society. This book bore not just the fruit of her prayer and reflection; it also drew deeply from her personal experience of the social ills that fell to the poor—mainly women— in the large cities of England as well as in the villages of Ireland. The publication of *Woman's Work in Modern Society* marked a decisive turning point in the life of this Irish Poor Clare nun and set the course for her vision of social activism.

In the preface to the book, she addresses men "who do not disdain to think,'' and asks of them a careful consideration of the subject of her work.

> I would appeal to that chivalrous courtesy which is certainly not yet dead in Old England. I would ask them, for the sake of their mothers, their sisters, and their wives, to treat the subject of Woman's destiny with the importance which it merits. To remember that women were not made to be the playthings of an idle hour, the toys of a wanton dalliance, the slaves of a selfish despotism.

And she challenges women: "I appeal to women; I beg of them to lay aside a little the sensational romance and to look stern facts in the face; for as surely as there is a sun in the heavens this day the future of England, the future of the world will be what women make it." The outline of her vision of social justice begins with the declaration that "all theories of life that are not founded on the true conditions of life must necessarily be defective." We must consider the conditions under which humanity exists before we can clearly understand the position of woman.

> Let the place and function of women be once clearly understood, and the ground of much prejudice and misapprehension is removed. Woman is, in right of her Creator, immortal and responsible. A thousand woes to him who dares to undermine her faith in her immortality, or to lessen her sense of her responsibility! These conditions of life belong to every woman, from the lady on her throne, who gives so rare an example of kindness to those who suffer in her service, down to the wretch who expiates her offences against society in the woes of penal servitude.

Sister Francis Clare drew attention to the conditions of women whose education was such that they remained ill-equipped to support themselves or to better the quality of their lives. She argued for higher wages for working women: "How many cases of suicide," she cried, "and how many cases of real, literal starvation arise from the greed which will not pay fair wages to the poor workwoman! How many girls are driven to a life which they abhor simply to get bread, the bread which is denied to them by those who squander on folly what is due to justice!" She saw clearly that injustices to women—in the kind of education and upbringing they received and in the unfair labor practices, particularly low pay, they were subjected to—were prime causes of social unrest, the break-up of families, the lack of peace in the world.

CONGREGATIONAL ARCHIVES

Correspondence in the congregational archives of the Sisters of Peace shows that in 1882, Sister Francis Clare tried to open an industrial school, putting into practice some of the elements of the theory propounded in *Woman's Work*, in the village of Knock, in Ireland. Meeting with opposition from various quarters, she responded to an invitation from the bishop of the industrial city of Nottingham, England, to come and establish her works of peace in his diocese. Sister Clare had, by this time, come to realize that the welfare of women, particularly working women, required practical action based on sound economic theory and carried out in faith for the kingdom of peace and justice. She was inspired by the signs of her time to found a new order of sisters who would provide education, practical training, and housing to women so as to encourage peace in families, in the church, and in the world. The manuscript copy of the first constitutions of the Sisters of Peace in the congregational archives sets forth clearly the mission of this new order: "The object of the institute is, as its name implies, to promote the peace of the Church, both by word and work. The very name Sisters of Peace will, it is hoped, even of itself, inspire the desire of peace and a love for it." And again: "My object is simple; it is to found a religious order devoted to the domestic training of girls." She elaborated the theory that had formed in her mind and heart ten years earlier:

> A great deal of the political disturbance of the present day arises from the social condition of the so-called lower classes. I have no utopian schemes for making millionaires of poor men (sic), I have a long-formed, very ardent desire to train the poor for domestic life in a practical way.

The 100 years since those first steps in social activism have served as testing ground for the vision of peace-making through practical action bequeathed to the Sisters of Peace by Margaret Anna Cusack. Archival documents record the attempts made by her followers to read the signs of *their* times in fidelity to the mission of peace through justice as articulated by the founder and officially sanctioned by the church.

THE FEMINIST PERSPECTIVE

The archival documents that describe the social-justice activities of the past 100 years tell another story, more subtly nuanced and perhaps more truly the expression of faithfulness to the vision outlined in Margaret Anna Cusack's *Woman's Work in Modern Society*. That story concerns the evolution in self-understanding of women religious as experienced by the Sisters of Peace. Research into the feminist perspective in the various works and ministries taken up by the Sisters of Peace throughout the century has meant looking at the data not in terms of "this work and that ministry" but as the story of women changing their social role from that of children to adults, from instruments to agents, from subjects to participants. It is a story characterized by the sisters' efforts to make peace in a society divided by sex discrimination and to move that society toward women's participation in decision-making. Seen from the perspective of women in quest of justice, such an account becomes HERstory rather than HIStory. In the HERstory, Margaret Anna Cusack is recalled as one of many charismatic leaders who had struggled long and hard to sensitize 19th- and 20th-century religious people to an awareness of the need to confront, in the name of religion, the pervasive structural indigence and oppression that accompanied the industrialization of Europe and the United States. Religious communities, especially communities of women, carried on this task but under the leadership of the Church hierarchy. The first constitutions of the Sisters of Peace spell out this relationship between the religious community and the bishop: "The Sisters shall carry out the great end for which this religious order is instituted by combining a life of interior recollection and prayer with such active works of charity as shall be deemed most necessary and advisable by the Ordinary of the diocese." This relationship conformed to the then-contemporary identification of women as means to an end, as instruments or as objects. Such was the situation in 1890. The archives show, however, that in 1978 the Sisters chose to set their own priorities in respect to their mission of working on behalf of the poor and powerless. They established a fund for sisters involved in urban ministry, drew up a plan to rehabilitate community-owned buildings for low- and moderate-income families, undertook research on the need for an urban, multi-dimensional alternative school, and sponsored a group home for children without families to care for them. The process by which the sisters arrived at the mature acceptance of responsibility that comes with acceptance of freedom parallels the evolution of women in society as a whole who recognized the disparities between them and their male counterparts in opportunities to compete equally for professional advancement, to receive equal salary for equal work, and especially to participate in the decision-making process. Women religious have taken heart from Pope John XXIII's encyclical *Pacem in Terris* in which he said: "Since women are becoming more conscious of their human dignity, they will not tolerate being treated as inanimate objects or mere instruments but claim, both in domestic and in public life, the rights and duties that befit a human person" (41). Vatican II's emphasis on freedom, subsidiarity, and collegiality moved the Sisters of Peace to recognize the power of the person as agent and to accept the responsibility, the initiative, and the leadership that this presumes. Chapter decrees from 1968 state the following:

> We resolve to do all in our power to support all minority groups in their struggle for equality and human dignity and to eradicate racism in our country and in the congregation. . . . We have this responsibility as Christians who are morally committed to love all, and as religious who have an obligation to take initiative and assume leadership.

The foregoing data suggest that religious women's archives offer a roadmap to the study of the evolution of women from "playthings of an idle hour," to quote Margaret Anna Cusack, to equal partners in the process of decision-making.

At this point, it is too much to hope that the "well-kept secret" of religious archives as reference resource has been exposed sufficiently to relegate it to the dankest, darkest recesses of the archival graveyard of unusable information?

This essay has outlined some factors that have prevented the reference librarian and researcher from availing themselves of the resources of the religious archive. It has described religious archives in general and then discussed the archives of women religious organizations, focusing on the excellent reference and research tool *Women Religious History Sources. A Guide to Repositories in the United States*. Next followed examples of archival research in religiously motivated social activism with respect to the related areas of women's issues and the changing perception of women religious. The secret is out—go tell the world!

Reference Service in Catholic Diocesan Archives

James M. O'Toole

As an institution, the Roman Catholic church has been generating and preserving archival records longer than any other. From the appointment of special notaries charged with collecting the acts and sayings of the martyrs at the end of the first century until the present day, the church has been creating records which document the role it has played in western civilization and the lives of millions of people. At the same time it has, with greater or lesser zeal, organized those records and made them available for study. In the United States this tradition is of much more recent historical vintage, but it still embraces the nearly two hundred years since the first Catholic diocese was organized at Baltimore in 1789. Today, dioceses across the country create and preserve the permanently valuable records of the Catholic experience in America.[1]

In recent years there has been a growing amount of interest in Catholic diocesan archives. Prompted initially by interest in the American Revolutionary bicentennial in the 1970s and now by the impending bicentennial of the appointment of John Carroll, the first American bishop, diocesan officials are devoting more attention to the care and use of their archives. Though in the past diocesan archives were frequently the step-children of church administration, presided over by well-meaning but untrained amateurs, with little access granted to outside researchers, increasing numbers of professional archival programs are now being established and are flourishing. These programs encompass the full range of archival functions, including records management, arrangement and description, reference service, and programs of education, outreach, and exhibit.[2]

Mr. O'Toole is the Archivist for the Catholic Archdiocese of Boston, 2121 Commonwealth Avenue, Brighton, Massachusetts 02135.

© 1986 by The Haworth Press, Inc. All rights reserved.

IMPETUS FOR RENEWED INTEREST

The impetus for all this activity can be traced to the "Document on Ecclesiastical Archives," issued in 1974 by the National Conference of Catholic Bishops, the principal national coordinating body for the church in the United States. This statement, which had been drafted by prominent Catholic historians and archivists, decried the too-frequent lack of concern for diocesan archives and the effect which that unconcern had had on the writing and study of American Catholic history. Clearly adopting the view that archival records are valuable only when they are used, the bishops' conference urged the appointment of a properly-trained archivist in every diocese in the country, even if only on a part-time basis. It also encouraged each bishop to grant access to diocesan archives "without undue limitations." Only in this way could historians penetrate "to the heart of the peculiarly American experience" and understand "the contributions of our forebears to the mission of the church and to the formation of the nation."[3]

The response to this call for greater attention to diocesan archives was encouragingly swift and broadly-based. From a handful of programs located in a few major dioceses (such as Baltimore, San Antonio, and Los Angeles), the number of diocesan archives grew dramatically. The 1961 *Guide to Archives and Manuscripts in the United States*, edited by Philip M. Hamer, had found only four diocesan archives among its survey of more than 1,300 American repositories. By 1978, when the National Historical Publications and Records Commission issued its *Directory of Archives and Manuscript Repositories in the United States*, that number had grown to thirty-four and was still expanding. In the spring of 1979, a meeting and workshop specifically for diocesan archivists attracted forty-five participants, representing more than one-quarter of all the dioceses in the country, a figure that at future meetings approached one-half. Since that time, the group has continued to meet annually, and in 1982 it formally organized itself into the Association of Catholic Diocesan Archivists.[4] Dioceses large and small, old and young, and stretching from Maine to California were devoting sustained attention to their archival records. Many diocesan archivists were religious, both male and female, but increasing numbers of professionally-trained lay people were attracted to the field. Coupled with a revival of interest in American Catholic history, in which researchers began to apply the methods and insights of social history to their work, the availability and use of diocesan archives has made accessible a great deal of previously-unused documentary material.

TYPES OF RECORDS

What kinds of records do diocesan archives contain and how do diocesan archivists assist those who want to use and study them? Regardless of its age or precise historical circumstances, every diocese tends to generate the same kinds of records through similar administrative structures.[5] These begin with the records and papers of the bishop himself. Such documents are comparable to the records of the chief executive officer of any large organization or governmental unit, with the addition of material deriving from the spiritual activities and functions of the bishop. One may find greater or lesser collections of letters, diaries, and other kinds of records, depending on the individual bishop's own personality and his dispositions as a record-keeper and record-preserver. In the nineteenth century, when diocesan administration was a relatively simple and more direct activity, the bishop handled most matters himself, with the result that a very rich documentary record was created. As time went on and various functions became the responsibility of particular offices and agencies, the bishop's own papers lost some of their all-inclusive nature, though they remain central to any diocesan archives collection.

It was that expanding church bureaucracy, especially in the first half of the twentieth century, which was the most significant generator of the records now held in diocesan archives. Some of these records derive from the operation and administration of canon law, including records of the reception of the sacraments, such as baptism, marriage, ordination, and anointing of the sick. Others derive from activities in civil law, including contracts and deeds to church property. Most derive from the routine financial, personnel, and general administrative activities that one would expect to find in such a large organization. These include correspondence files, blueprints, budgets, and other material relating to the management of the parishes, schools, hospitals, social welfare agencies, and other institutions affiliated with the diocese. These administrative records were all created to accomplish some specific current (and occasionally mundane) purpose, but with the passage of time they take on additional value as historical sources. Not all of them—not even the majority—are permanently valuable; appraising these records and discarding those without long-term usefulness remains the most important thing a diocesan archivist, like any archivist, does.[6] Still, those records that remain after the appraisal process is complete become crucial to any diocesan archives.

Beyond these, many dioceses seek to preserve the records of parishes, institutions, and individuals by centralizing them in the diocesan archives. Parish baptismal and marriage registers; church bulletins and pulpit announcement books; the entrance and discharge records of orphanages and homes; minute books, membership lists, and other records of organizations of the laity; personal papers of priests, nuns, and prominent lay people—all can be found in diocesan archives. This material may take a variety of forms, embracing traditional manuscripts and typescripts, still and motion pictures, sound recordings, computer records, and even some artifacts. Though many archives are founded to care for the documents of central diocesan administration, these records do not stand alone in providing evidence about church life. Accordingly, most diocesan archives recognize their responsibility to preserve local Catholic history not only from the top down but also from the bottom up. In defining the scope of their collecting policies as broadly as possible, these archives work toward a fuller documentation of a church that has, in the last twenty years, taken the democratic phrase "people of God" as the primary metaphor of its character.

The ways in which diocesan archives care for this material and assist those who seek to use it do not differ substantially from the comparable goals and procedures in other archives and libraries, both religious and secular. Because many diocesan archives have been founded only recently, their first responsibility is frequently to conduct an initial survey or inventory of their holdings. All other archival tasks depend on the achieving of a fundamental level of intellectual control over the collection. If some diocesan archives have in the past been reluctant to grant access to their materials, it has been the result of the absence of this basic intellectual control as much as a desire for secrecy. By identifying the existing holdings of the diocesan archives, as well as adding new material through the application of records management techniques that preserve the non-current records of working offices, the diocesan archivist is able to answer the primary question about the collection: "what material is here?" Then, by producing a variety of finding aids—inventories, registers, catalogs, guides, and so on—the archivist makes the reference process possible. Once the collection is identified and adequately described, it is possible to locate its points of intersection with the topical interest of individual researchers.

ROLE OF THE REFERENCE INTERVIEW

Any archivist or librarian would find most of the reference procedures in diocesan archives entirely recognizable. The centerpiece of these procedures is the reference interview, whether formal or informal, in which both the archivist and the researcher determine how the collection can be used to best advantage. In this interview, the archivist is interested in learning the subject matter of the researcher's investigation and the kind of information that is being sought. As a part of this, it is important to know what other repositories and sources, whether published or unpublished, have already been consulted or which the researcher intends to examine in the future. Not infrequently this requires the archivist to help the researcher articulate the real question he or she wants to ask, and it offers the opportunity to pass along knowledge about other collections or similar studies which may be unknown but which will also bear on the subject at hand. Finally, the archivist can outline the particular collections that will warrant the researcher's investment of time and energy, as well as the various descriptive media that allow entry directly into their contents.

From the researcher's point of view, the reference interview also accomplishes several important goals. It provides the opportunity to discuss the research project with a sympathetic listener who may be able to offer a different perspective on it, as well as the chance to get a more detailed sense of the contents of the collection than is available merely from the written guides or finding aids. Because most diocesan archives remain small, one- or two-person operations, the reference archivist will also in many cases have been the processing archivist. Thus, the archivist may retain some knowledge about the coverage, strengths, and weaknesses of the papers that has not found its way into the formal finding aids. (Obviously, in producing those finding aids, the archivist has an obligation to keep such oversights to a minimum.) Similarly, the archivist may know but have forgotten about related subjects or complementary uses of the material, and the researcher can jog this memory. Finally, the researcher may have been able to locate or identify important collections of records not yet under archival control, thereby assisting the archivist in the future development of the collection.

TYPICAL USERS

These aspects of the reference process in diocesan archives would be entirely recognizable in almost any other kind of archives. There are, however, several ways in which reference service in diocesan archives is different from that in other repositories. The first of these stems from the high volume of use these collections can receive and the wide variety of that use. In a typical recent year in the Archives of the Archdiocese of Boston, for example, we have responded to more than 3,000 requests for information from the records and documents in the collection. Almost 40 percent of these come as a result of personal visits to our research room; another 40 percent result from telephone inquiries, and the remainder come through the mail. This averages a rate of between twelve and thirteen each day, of which four or five entail use of the material in person. Such a steady volume clearly places demands on the limited staff, consisting of two full-time professional archivists and one half-time clerical assistant. Nonetheless, the volume is an encouraging one because it means that the collection is being preserved not merely for its own sake, but so that it can be used.

Even more significant than simple volume of use is the range of subject interests on the part of the users and the number of different backgrounds they bring to their use of the archives. Though many diocesan archives owe their creation as a separate department to a legitimate interest in local church history, historical scholarship generally accounts for only a small proportion of research use. Far more significant is the use of the archives by diocesan administrators. Whether from chancellors who, in resolving currently pending issues, need precedents and background information from correspondence files; accountants and other financial administrators who seek data on the management of temporal affairs; engineers who require blueprints and construction documents to assist them in maintaining church, school, and hospital buildings; attorneys who need to have access to contracts, wills, and land deeds; pastors who seek previous canonical and sacramental records to serve their flocks—all of these will need to draw on the resources of the diocesan archives. Very few of these users think of themselves as researchers or as "reference patrons" in the traditional sense. They are, however, regular users of the diocesan archives, and the archivist must provide them with helpful, efficient reference service. If anything, the diocesan archivist will make an extra effort to help such people since they are related more closely to the archives than outside researchers; in many cases they are the people who "pay the bills."

Researchers from outside diocesan structure cannot be slighted, and of these, genealogists are usually the most numerous. They seek to understand the long tradition of the church and what it has meant to thousands of people, both in groups and as individuals. Family researchers have come increasingly to draw on church records as they seek to reconstruct their own and related families. This occurs not only because public vital records sometimes do not exist, but also because the church records provide different kinds of information. The godparents whose names are recorded with a child's baptism, for example, may be clues pointing in the direction of uncles, aunts, and other members of the extended family—subjects on which the public records are silent. Interest in genealogical research has broadened considerably in recent years beyond its narrow base among those old families of English stock. Genealogy has "gone ethnic," and that extends to many people whose immigrant ancestors had longstanding associations with the Catholic church.[7] For these researchers the diocesan archives can be a crucial resource.

TREND TOWARD PEOPLE HISTORY

Historical scholarship remains important, and the use of diocesan archives in writing American Catholic history has grown, an increase resulting from several factors. First, as more archives are established and organize their materials, historians are discovering large quantities of primary sources that have been either unexamined altogether or under-utilized. What is more, the increasing tendency of Catholic historians to write social or "people history" leads them to seek information not only about the church's leadership elites, but also about the average men and women in the pews.[8] Scholars researching such topics as the growth of parochial school systems, the development and role of church-related charitable and social welfare institutions, the role of religious sisters, the activities of organizations of lay people, and the changing nature of popular belief and devotional life can find large collections of previously unstudied records in diocesan archives.

The impact of this variety of research in diocesan archives on the reference process is direct, if somewhat complex. It means that finding aids and other guides need to be constructed with a maximum amount of flexibility. Since it is possible—even likely—that many different researchers will all look at the same records with different purposes in mind, the finding aids will have to accommodate and make as easy as possible those different uses. More important, the varieties of use in diocesan archives means that the archivist will face widely diverging levels of research experience and ability. Some users (though probably not a majority) will be experienced researchers who come to the archives well prepared and with specific questions in mind. Others will be walking into an archives of any kind for the first time in their lives, with all the uncertainties and lack of knowledge, but generally with keen interest and good will, that implies. Like the reference librarian in a public library, therefore, the diocesan archivist must be ready for all comers, ready to meet the researcher where he or she is, and be willing to help. Some researchers will need more help than others; some may be exasperating. If the archives is to be truly accessible, however, these differences will have to be accommodated.

Related to this diversity is a second way in which reference work in a diocesan archives may differ from that in other repositories. Because the materials in the collection can support such a divergence of research, the diocesan archivist may discover a shifting boundary line between current information and historical or archival information. The same records can, often surprisingly, change from one characteristic to the other. The records of a one-hundred-year-old church, for example, including blueprints, original drawings, financial records, pew rents, and sacramental registers, may be preserved in the archives because of their historical importance. They can be studied by art and architectural historians, by historians of particular ethnic groups, and by genealogists for the information they contain about life, religion, and culture in the past. Should the church be damaged by fire, however, or its roof need repair, the same records take on a more pressing importance in addressing very real problems of today. What had been historical and past becomes current and pressing. The archivist must be prepared for such swift changes in the uses of diocesan records, both by the flexible construction of finding aids and by developing the ability to look at the same records from several different perspectives at once. In providing reference service, all archivists must be able to put themselves, to a greater or lesser extent, in the researcher's shoes. In diocesan archives, as the church's past can rapidly become its present, this is a doubly important skill.

DOCUMENTING THE INTANGIBLE

Finally, reference service in diocesan archives may differ from that in other archives which do not have a religious foundation because of the unusual nature of what it is that they seek to document. Religious archivists of all kinds, across the many denominational lines, are coming to realize that theirs is a peculiarly difficult task. Like the archivists of other, secular institutions, they seek to preserve evidence and information about an institution for its own benefit and that of others. Religious institutions are different, however, because they believe that that hard, physical, institutional reality is not the only one—indeed, not the most important one. Religious archivists are faced with the added responsibility of helping to document something very intangible and therefore difficult to capture: religious faith and belief.[9] Any religious institution, including a Catholic diocese, exists to foster and promote such an intangible, and its archives must therefore seek to preserve its traces, no matter how hard they may be to find. Though there are similarities, the archives of a religious organization like a diocese must be more than the archives of General Motors or that of a similar institution. Neither the business archivist nor the researcher in those collections will, as a general rule, be interested in the "spirit" of the company or the supernatural values it promoted. For religious archivists, those concerns will always lie just beneath the surface.

Thus, in a diocesan archives, the archivist must be ready to preserve, organize, and make available records that would perhaps not be judged particularly valuable in another setting. At the same time, the archives may be in the position of trying to help researchers answer questions that do not normally get asked of other institutional records. What did the people of this church believe about God, themselves, and the world, and what difference did it make in their lives? How did their activities and societies reflect those beliefs? How, if at all, did they record their feelings, whether in writing or in other audio-visual media? Researchers in diocesan archives will want to see through the documentation of practical things and gain insight into the moving spirit behind them, the higher reality they reflect. Diocesan archivists must aid in that process, both by what they collect and by how they help people use that material.

This requires a certain amount of natural sympathy on the part of the archivist, or at least a willingness to accept such inquiries as legitimate. It also involves the archivist in an interesting and exciting quest, an inquiry to which there may be no final or fully satisfactory answers. "No one has ever seen God," as St. John's gospel reminds us. In helping others use the collections in their care, diocesan archivists may be able to provide glimpses of His actions and those of His people in the very real world in which we all live.

---

1. A diocese is a geographical unit of organization, based roughly on population, and comprised of many local parishes. Each diocese is centered in the major city of its region, and is presided over by a bishop, who is its chief spiritual and temporal administrator. An archdiocese is merely a kind of diocese whose archbishop exercises very general supervisory authority over neighboring bishops and dioceses.

2. Recent developments in this field are summarized in James M. O'Toole, "Catholic Diocesan Archives: A Renaissance in Progress." *American Archivist* 43 (1980): 284-293, and Peter J. Wosh, "Keeping the Faith? Bishops, Historians, and Catholic Diocesan Archivists, 1790-1980." *Midwestern Archivist* 9 (1984): 15-26.

3. National Conference of Catholic Bishops, *A Document on Ecclesiastical Archives.* Washington, D.C.: NCCB, 1974.

4. Many of these developments are described in greater detail in O'Toole, "Catholic Diocesan Archives."

5. Francis J. Weber described the holdings of one pioneer diocesan archives, that for the archdiocese of Los Angeles, in "Chancery Archives," *American Archivist* 28 (1965): 255-260. For more recent descriptions of the typical holdings of such repositories, see Barnabas Diekemper, *Guide to the Catholic Archives at San Antonio* (San Antonio: Archdiocese of San Antonio, 1978) and James M. O'Toole, *Guide to the Archives of the Archdiocese of Boston* (New York: Garland, 1982). See also Francis J. Weber, "Printed Guides to Archival Centers for American Catholic History." *American Archivist* 32 (1969): 349-356.

6. The larger questions, both theoretical and practical, of records appraisal have come increasingly to occupy the attention of archival thinkers. For a summary of this thought see the essays in Nancy E. Peace, ed. *Archival Choices: Managing the Historical Record in an Age of Abundance.* Lexington, Mass.: Lexington Books, 1983.

7. For more information on this, see James M. O'Toole, "Catholic Church Records: A Genealogical and Historical Resource" *New England Historical and Genealogical Register* 132 (1978): 251-263.

8. The first systematic attempt to incorporate this broadened perspective into Catholic history is James Hennesey, *American Catholics; A History of the Roman Catholic Community in the United States.* New York: Oxford University Press, 1981.

9. The seminal article on this unusual responsibility is Robert Shuster, "Documenting the Spirit." *American Archivist* 45 (1982): 135-141.

Establishing an Image: The Role of Reference Service in a New Archival Program

Thomas Wilsted

The Salvation Army was founded in England in 1865 by William Booth. Its primary goals were saving souls and providing for the religious needs of the poor in the East End of London. However, Booth soon learned that those without food or shelter were not receptive to the Christian message. The Salvation Army soon adopted programs to aid the poor including inexpensive meals and shelters where the Army could serve man's spiritual and physical needs.

Booth's Army spread quickly throughout England and then abroad when a contingent of overseas missionaries, consisting of seven women and one man, arrived in New York City in 1880. With headquarters first in Philadelphia and later in New York, The Salvation Army quickly achieved comparable success in the United States. By 1883, the Army was established on both the East and West coasts and inroads were slowly made into the interior. As the organization grew, it developed shelters for the homeless, rescue homes for prostitutes, maternity hospitals for unwed mothers, farm colonies, alcohol and drug rehabilitation programs, and day care and community centers.

IMPETUS FOR A NEW ARCHIVAL PROGRAM

Although its history in the United States began in 1880, The Salvation Army did not seriously begin to preserve its documentary heritage until 1973, the tenth decade of its existence in the U.S. By then, approaching its centennial year, it had grown to a movement operating in four territories covering all fifty states, and staffed by 5,000 officers (ordained ministers), and 26,000 employees.[1] In

---

The author is Archivist/Administrator at the Salvation Army Archives and Research Center, 145 West 15th Street, New York, New York 10011.

© 1986 by The Haworth Press, Inc. All rights reserved.

1973, the second in command of the Eastern Territory, Chief Secretary Colonel John Waldron, appointed the first Historical Commission. The avowed purpose of this group was to encourage an interest in the organization's history in the hope that this would lead to the establishment of an archival program.

The nucleus of the archival collection was material from the Literary Department, including Salvation Army publications, photographs, and a miscellaneous collection of archival records. During 1974, the first clerical staff was appointed to care for the collection. Over the next three years, Army representatives met with archival consultants Shonnie Finnegan and Andrea Hinding. As a result of their discussions, one floor of a Salvation Army building was renovated for archival use. It was agreed that the Archives would serve all of the United States, not just the eleven northeastern states of the Eastern Territory, and that a professional archival staff would be employed. This was accomplished by mid-1978 when The Salvation Army Archives and Research Center was formally dedicated, two years before the Army's centennial celebration.

The development of the Archives and Research Center was due in great part to the leadership of Colonel Waldron and his successor, Colonel Norman S. Marshall. However, because the Archives and Research Center began as an Eastern Territorial project, its services and purpose were virtually unknown among Salvation Army personnel in other parts of the United States. This fact, combined with a lack of understanding of archival programs generally, was a serious obstacle to the new archives program.

Once the professional staff was employed, its first concern was to publicize the archives program and establish its image. Because the Archives is part of a larger organization, every effort was made to provide useful services and become an information resource for Salvation Army officers and employees. While reference service would clearly be an important method of establishing an archival image of institutional usefulness, this service began slowly because of the lack of finding aids and intellectual control over the collection.

SETTING REFERENCE POLICIES

When the Archives and Research Center was established, it was believed that it would be used primarily by Salvation Army personnel but that it would also be open for research by the public. To make the collection as usable as possible by a wide audience, the Archives sought few restrictions on access.

It was agreed that all published and audio-visual material would be available without restriction as to the age of the researcher or the research purpose. However, access to official Salvation Army records posed a number of serious questions. The Archives often receives very recent records, some of which are sensitive or relate to ongoing programs. In addition, it holds many types of confidential records which may be made available only to certain personel or released under specific guidelines. These include personnel records, social welfare case records, minutes of board meetings, and similar material. After discussion with members of the Advisory Committee of the Archives and Research Center, a policy was drafted stating that archival records less than twenty-five years old are available only to researchers with the approval of the head of the Archives and the head of the department which created the records.[2] Records more than twenty-five years old are available to researchers without needing approval unless a specific restriction has been requested by the transferring department. This policy has proved practical, easy to understand and easy to monitor. The number of exceptions to the standard policy is not large. Any restriction placed on material such as case records is agreed on by the Archives and the transferring department at the time the material is placed in the Archives & Research Center, avoiding future misunderstanding or disagreement.

While the access policy for official records was clear and precise, private papers donated by individuals posed a more difficult problem. In theory, donors are free to place whatever restrictions they feel are necessary. Because the Army has numerous families which have served in the officer ranks for three or four generations, some donors were concerned about what their ancestors might have said about the ancestor of a friend or acquaintance. This concern about privacy, even with records approaching one hundred years in age, caused the Archives to walk a narrow line between access and the rights of individual donors. While donors were encouraged to place as few restrictions as possible, the Archives was forced to accept a new perception of privacy. In most cases, restrictions have been minor and justified. To ensure future unrestricted access to papers, the Archives makes every attempt to gain literary as well as property rights to collections so that control over access and publication resides with The Salvation Army.

Researchers are provided with photocopies and photographic prints of material in the Archives and Research Center at a nominal charge. The publication of a photograph requires the permission of the Archives, although there is no publication charge. The researcher is required to give a credit line for each photograph and to place copies of published works containing photographic reproductions in the Archives and Research Center for future reference.

DEVELOPMENT OF FINDING AIDS

While policies on access and copying were being adopted, the Archives staff began planning the collection's finding aids for use by researchers. The plans included a multi-level system consisting of a card catalog, archives and manuscript collection inventories, and indexes to some archival collections and to periodicals. It was thought that these finding aids would be used both by researchers and Archives staff, so all planning emphasized simplicity and ease of access.

A card catalog is the first point of reference for researchers. All material, regardless of format, is to be included. Each entry has author, title, and subject cards. To make each type of material easier to find, the Archives adopted a system of color-coded cards: white—books, red—photographs, green—archives, blue—pamphlets, etc. This feature has proved especially useful when searches involve a subject with a large number of entries in a particular archival format such as photographs. While the catalog led researchers to particular items or collections, the Archives needed more detailed inventories for its archives and manuscripts. The inventory consists of two parts: a cover sheet containing basic details about the collection and a box and folder listing. For smaller collections, the cover sheet fully describes the collection and gives the box and folder listings. Larger collections may also include scope and content notes as well as a history or chronology of the department or operating unit.

While most collections were adequately described using standard finding aids, a number of collections required detailed indexing to make them readily accessible. Collections of personnel records and social service case records contained thousands of individual files and without an index were virtually useless. In such cases, name indexes were developed which refer the researcher to a specific box and folder or to a particular microfilm reel.

The Archives and Research Center evaluated its reference experience after the first few years of operation. It found that internal inquiries were quite specific and certain types of information were needed, which could usually be found in periodicals or archives collections. However, this required considerable searching on the part of the reference staff. If the Archives was going to foster an image of usefulness without spending enormous amounts of time on each reference question, then indexes were needed. A set of standard subject terms was developed, based on Salvation Army activities and terminology. Using these terms, the staff began the slow and tedious process of indexing various Army periodicals. Work began with several small social service periodicals published in the late 19th and early 20th centuries to test the subject terms and to develop procedures for use in future indexing projects. Three periodicals are now completed and work will begin on a thorough indexing of *The War Cry*, the weekly newspaper begun in 1881, sometime in 1985.

The indexes have proved to be a boon to researchers. They have provided an immense amount of data previously unavailable because of being submerged in the periodicals. It has made reference work easier and has pleased the many researchers who have benefitted from its availability. Index entries to the three periodicals plus an inherited, incomplete index to *The War Cry* currently total 66,000 entries.

In addition to the finding aids, the Archives & Research Center established three sets of vertical files for reference use. There is a biographical file, a general subject file on activities and programs, and an institutional file. The files contain such items as histories of individual operating units, newspaper clippings, lists of Salvation Army officers, addresses where Army programs are located, and ephemera.

The vertical files store data which are too small to catalog although they provide ready access for reference use. Such items as funeral programs and building dedication booklets provide historical information often found nowhere else. At the same time, some subject files, such as Salvation Army involvement in World War I or biographical files on leading Salvationists, are fairly voluminous and can be used by researchers who require specific data but do not have time for extended research.

The finding aids described above are based on standard archival and library models and employ the use of typed inventories, indexes, and catalog cards. The only automation available has been an electronic typewriter with a 2-1/2 page memory. This is used primarily to reproduce catalog cards since the use of color-coded cards precludes reproduction by photo-duplication. While this system has proved adequate, the application of computer technology could shorten many procedures and make finding aids more effective.

In late 1984, The Salvation Army began planning for the introduction of microcomputers into many installations. The Archives and Research Center presented a case for its needs and in November, 1984, an IBM PC XT with twenty megabytes of hard disk storage was placed in the Archives. The machine came complete with word processing software and is already being used for the input, storage, and updating of archival finding aids. After investigating a number of data processing packages designed for archives and libraries, the Archives purchased an INMAGIC software package. At the present time the Archives is designing programs for inputting, storage, and retrieval of periodical indexes, with the capability for handling such diverse material as books, photographs, archives, and manuscripts. The system is extremely flexible and, with minor programming, will be a rapid, cost-effective means of retrieving information from material throughout the collection.

ENCOURAGING THE USE OF REFERENCE SERVICE

While not every archives attempts to establish an image reflecting its collections and activities, many do. The image they reflect may be of the building they occupy, the material in their collection, or the services they provide. The image may be a reflection of when the archives was established or the type of institution of which it is a part. A young, institutional archives faces a number of problems in establishing an image: it starts out with a small and usually limited collection, does not have its own building and may have only a few rooms within its institutional headquarters, is closely identified with its own institution, and has no history upon which to build.

The directors of new archives have a range of choices in image-making and, in many cases, choose to emphasize the acquisition of large or especially important collections as a means of identifying their new archives. While collections certainly cannot be ignored, the Archives and Research Center instead chose the course of providing a wide range of services to its institution as its image-building tool, with reference service as one of the most important components.

As soon as the Archive and Research Center developed adequate intellectual control and finding aids for its collection, efforts were begun to encourage reference use. Articles appeared in *The War Cry* and other Salvation Army periodicals indicating the services available to researchers. The Archives newsletter promoted the use of material in the collection, indicating the types of material and information available. The Archives invited departmental representatives to a workshop in the Archives to discover more about the reference services available and to learn through hands-on experience how to use them.

Researchers in colleges and universities were not forgotten. Information about reference service and collections was announced in *The American Archivist* and in scholarly journals. Lists of potential topics for which there was adequate research material in the Archives were compiled and these were distributed to colleges and universities in the New York City area.

Although the Archives has not produced displays specifically on reference service, displays do make the Archives better known and indirectly encourage reference inquiries. The Archives and Research Center made a consistent effort to develop both internal and external displays from its inception. They range from small, traveling displays designed for The Salvation Army centennial to lobby window displays to larger displays for use in conjunction with Army conventions.

While it is hard to measure the effectiveness of displays on research use, those staffed by Archives personnel were indicative. They provided an opportunity to discuss the archives program with visitors. When the discussions elicited questions from individuals, they found in the Archives an institution which could provide answers. From this experience, it was learned that some persons have questions but are too busy to take time to write a letter. To overcome this problem, a reference form was developed for use with displays. The inquirer could provide his/her name and address and then list the subject or person about whom they needed information. Quite a number of people visiting the displays filled out this form and were sent information in response to their queries.

While efforts to promote reference service are effective, there is a strong feeling among the staff that good reference service itself is important in establishing an image of usefulness and increasing reference use. Good reference service consists of a number of important components. It is important that researchers feel welcome and that the reference archivist is courteous and helpful whether the inquiry comes by telephone, letter, or a personal visit. Since many people have never before used an archives, they are often apprehensive and do not know what to expect. A pleasant reception is important in putting people at ease and allowing them to frame their questions in such a way that the Archives can be of help. Comments made by users of the Archives indicate pleasure at the friendly and courteous reception and this may well be a factor in repeated usage.

While this is important in image building, providing the information or material to researchers is of equal or greater value. Although clearly a question cannot be answered if the information is not available in the Archives collection, when information is available, it must reach the researchers. While this statement seems straightforward, the Archives staff has found that sometimes researchers do not always know exactly what kind of information they need, and it must help to clarify the question. Researchers sometimes call and ask the Archives to send everything on a particular town or subject. When asked how they plan to use the material, their response indicates that certain, specific pieces of information will provide the data needed for a speech or an article being written. However, without this careful probing, researchers might not receive the information they need or might receive more data than they could digest.

A final factor in good reference service is that researchers receive the information they require promptly and in time for any deadlines they have to meet. Since most of the requests come by letter or telephone, one of the first questions to researchers is, "When do you need this?" The Archives makes every effort to meet their deadlines, and if special photographic service or overnight mail is required, these are arranged with the understanding that researchers will bear these extra charges.

As we see repeat letters from inquirers, find people being referred by former researchers, and receive letters of thanks, there is a feeling that good service is more than its own reward. Clearly, it is another means of developing and encouraging reference service.

ARCHIVAL OUTREACH AND REFERENCE SERVICES

While reference service has been traditionally considered the providing of information in response to requests by researchers, an archives often contains specialized information or expertise which it can and should make available even if not solicited. Since the Archives and Research Center was interested in developing an image of institutional usefulness, it enthusiastically developed a number of programs of "archival outreach." These programs offered information available only in the Archives and, in the long run, encouraged additional reference inquiries.

One type of specialized expertise which an archives can provide is information and training in records management. Soon after the Archives and Research Center was established, the staff began a program to survey Salvation Army records and develop a records manual and record retention schedules. While the program was designed to benefit the Archives, it had value to The Salvation Army as a whole since it resulted in clearing storage area of unwanted records, saved the cost of buying expensive filing equipment, and introduced new technology such as microfilm. However, the program had an important side effect on the Archives. Since the survey was done by visiting Salvation Army installations throughout the United States, it was possible to explain the archives program in person and this elicited many reference inquiries.

Records management is only one of the areas of expertise found in an archives. Most archives are concerned about the conservation of their collections. Even if they do not have a conservator on their staff, archivists have developed an understanding and knowledge of conservation procedures and preventive measures. As the result of a recent visit by a conservation consultant, the Archives and Research Center became especially aware of the need for disaster planning. The archivists found in collecting information, that the data would be equally valuable to Salvation Army units throughout the United States which might face fire, flood, or other disasters which could affect their current records.

As a result, the Archives and Research Center developed a brief manual covering disaster prevention, first steps in dealing with the disaster, and a list of names, addresses, and telephone numbers where expert assistance is available.[3] Through notices in the Archives' newsletter and other Army publications, requests for this information were received not only from Salvation Army units but from fire departments, other archives, and a variety of persons needing this assistance. Since the release of this information, the Archives has provided additional material from how to put together a scrapbook which will not further damage the photographs and letters it contains to specific questions such as, "What should I do with the Bible I dropped in the sink?'' Such information provides a useful service and extends the concept of archival reference.

Finally, the Archives often has facts it can share with Army members' institutional publications. Over the past several years in answering reference requests, the Archives staff has come across interesting pieces of information, such as Salvation Army "firsts" and similar data. Since it was felt that such information would be helpful to the editors of Army periodicals and newsletters, the Archives compiled several articles and paragraphs of varying lengths. These were distributed and found a ready market. Since the first distribution, requests for similar types of information on specific subjects have been received, indicating that there is a need for this type of reference service.

PROVIDING REFERENCE SERVICE

As indicated previously, the Archives and Research Center provides reference service to both a Salvation Army constituency and the public. Salvation Army requests make up 60-65% of the total and the remainder come from scholars, genealogists, and others. Army reference inquiries come from throughout the United States and from overseas. The largest number come from the northeastern part of the United States since the Archives is best known in this area and is most accessible for personal visits. Most inquiries come either by letter (47%) or telephone (39%) with the remainder being actual visits to the Archives.[4]

Salvation Army reference inquiries cover a variety of topics. Since The Salvation Army was founded in the United States in 1880, many Army programs are nearing their 100th anniversary and this provides a number of inquiries. Approximately 20% are related to a centennial or other anniversary being celebrated in a local corps (church) or institution. Other inquiries range from information for speeches to copies of photographs for Army publications to assistance with information and visual materials for television programs.

Another strong interest is research into family history. Many Salvation Army officers have three or four generations of ancestors who were also officers and are anxious to know more about their careers and activities. Because the Archives collection contains personnel and biographical subject files, photographs, and indexes to several periodicals, the reference staff is usually able to provide a detailed description of a person's career, activities, and publications.

Only a small percentage of reference requests come from the scholarly community although these requests are often more detailed and the researcher needs a wider variety and greater volume of material. Topics have included: the Salvation Army Farm Colonies, (a plan to move city dwellers back to farms), a comparison of the development of The Salvation Army in France and the United States, a history of the New York Staff Band, a history of Salvation Army work in Cincinnati, and a history of homes for unwed mothers in Cleveland. To meet their research needs, scholars drew primarily on archival records, periodicals, books, and photographs.

An interesting array of requests comes from persons staging plays or television programs in which Salvation Army officers appear. Many requests concern characters in the plays *Major Barbara* and *Guys and Dolls*. Stage and costume designers review photographs and illustrations to plan their costumes and sets. In their concern for detail, they often want to know the exact design of an Army crest or shield to guarantee authenticity.

The Archives is not immune to the inquiries of genealogists from around the United States seeking information about their ancestors. Requests can be very specific if coming from an experienced genealogist or very general, such as, "I have this photograph of my grandfather in a Salvation Army uniform. What can you tell me about him?" Nearly all of these requests come by mail and the reference staff uses personnel files, Army publications, books, and subject files in answering them. Although genealogists make up only a small percentage of reference inquiries, they are some of the most appreciative users.

EVALUATING REFERENCE SERVICES

Because of the importance the Archives and Research Center places on service to researchers, accurate and detailed statistics are maintained as a means of evaluating institutional progress. Information is reported both monthly and annually on the number of inquiries. These are broken down by how the inquiry was received and its source: whether it comes from within the Salvation Army or not and, if it is a Salvation Army inquiry, from what area of the country. The latter is particularly important since the Archives and

Research Center receives funds from The Army's four United States territories. Although a majority of inquiries still come from the Eastern Territory, the Archives tracks inquiries from the other territories and has made efforts during the past three years to encourage all territories to use the resources and facilities available.

In addition to the source of inquiries, the Archives also records the type of material used to answer reference inquiries. When members of the reference staff answer a telephone or mail inquiry, they use a reference form on which they record the sources they consult and the information they find. This form serves three functions: it serves as a checklist to ensure that all resources are reviewed, it can be referred to at a later date if the same question occurs or the researcher later calls for additional information and, finally, it can be used for compiling statistics on what types of material are used and which best answers different types of questions. From statistics recorded over the past two years, it has been found that approximately one-third of the questions were answered using Army periodicals. Archives and manuscripts were used for over 20% and books answered approximately 10% of the inquiries.[5] The recording of such statistics has been invaluable in determining where arrangement and indexing efforts should be placed and long-range planning also reflects this information.

Although only a small percentage of inquiries come from persons visiting the Archives, each researcher completes a reader's register and the reference staff conducts researcher interviews. The reader's register requests basic information such as the researcher's name, home and university or business address, the topic of study, and publication plans. The interview is important in learning more specifically about the researcher's topic. From this information, we can often suggest the types of material which would be helpful. Often, the interview will indicate the level of research which is being done and suggestions can be made on whether more or less detailed material would be helpful in a particular project.

An interview after the completion of research helps the Archives to assess how well we have met the researcher's expectations. Discussions indicate whether or not the researcher found the information he/she needed and whether the reference service was satisfactory. The Archives attempts to keep in touch with researchers doing in-depth projects and will send them additional information should material be uncovered as collections are processed or indexed.

PLANS FOR THE FUTURE

In both short and long-range plans, reference service will remain of central importance in the overall archives program. The computer will certainly play a role in the development of the Archives' finding aids and reference service. As the computer programs are written and the data entered, retrieval of information should become more accurate and retrieval time quicker. Already, the Archives is finding one computer will not serve all of our needs since it is used for the input of data, word processing, and reference searching. Plans for the future call for the linking of several PCs together through an IBM AT computer with the expectation that other Salvation Army units could gain access to our database over telephone lines.

The quality of reference service continues to be a principal concern. Because only a small percentage of persons visit the Archives for research, it is difficult to know whether researcher expectations are being met. Beginning this year, a questionnaire will be sent to a percentage of the researchers who used the Archives' reference service in 1984. They will be asked whether their information needs were met, whether the information or material they needed arrived on time, whether the reference service met their expectations, and how the reference services might be improved. Through this survey and similar efforts, the Archives hopes to maintain a level of excellence in reference service.

As new archives programs are started, each must select from a range of choices as it faces a new and uncertain future. Each must develop its collection, assure its preservation, and provide for a reasonable level of access. While different programs will put a stronger emphasis on one goal or another, experience at The Salvation Army Archives and Research Center seems to indicate that reference service, in all its aspects, is crucially important in an institutional archival setting. Through a continued effort to establish an image of usefulness through its reference services, the archives can establish its validity and role in the organization of which it is a part.

END NOTES

1. The Salvation Army Eastern Territory, *Disposition of Forces*, New York, 1984, p. 144.

2. The Salvation Army Eastern Territory, *Policy and Procedure Minute: Access of Records to Researchers*. September 7, 1982.

3. The Salvation Army Archives and Research Center. *Salvaging and Preserving Fire and Water Damaged Records: A Manual.* New York, 1983.
4. The Salvation Army Archives and Research Center, *Annual Report—1983*. New York, p. 8.
5. Ibid.

"What Do You Have on Arthur Flegenheimer?" Research and Reference at the Franklin D. Roosevelt Library

Raymond Teichman

The name Arthur Flegenheimer may be unfamiliar to all but specialists in criminal history, but this type of inquiry about obscure individuals is not an unusual one for the staff of the Franklin D. Roosevelt Library. To the archivists at this, the first of the presidential libraries, founded in 1940 by President Roosevelt himself, such inquiries are routine, sandwiched in between letters from scholars seeking what is available on the Pearl Harbor attack and fourth grade students urgently hunting for copies of everything on the Great Depression. As it turns out, the information on Mr. Flegenheimer, alias "Dutch Schultz," is easily located in the diaries of Henry Morgenthau, Jr. by using the subject card index created by Mr. Morgenthau's secretary and presently available in the Library's Research Room. This paper will examine how archivists prepare and make available to researchers the Library's resources and attempt to answer similar inquiries.

THE ROOSEVELT LEGACY

President Roosevelt established the Library to house the vast quantity of papers, books, memorabilia, photographs and audiovisual materials he had acquired over a lifetime of public service and

---

Mr. Teichman is Supervisory Archivist at the Franklin D. Roosevelt Library, National Archives and Records Administration, in Hyde Park, New York, 12538.

© 1986 by The Haworth Press, Inc. All rights reserved.

private collecting. He hoped the Library would become an important research center where scholars and the public would find preserved intact the records of his presidency and those of his associates. He entrusted the care of the building and its contents to the Archivist of the United States and his staff. Following the major reorganization of the federal bureaucracy in 1949, the Roosevelt Library, together with its parent organization the National Archives and Records Service, became part of the General Services Administration, a tie which was severed in April 1985. Since those early years when President Roosevelt himself ordered that materials be forwarded to Hyde Park to the present day, the archivists have endeavored to carry out the President's wishes and maintain this institution as an outstanding research center.

Over the past 44 years the Library has accessioned and processed over 200 collections whose 16 million pages help to document the events of the Depression and World War II, the lives of Franklin and Eleanor Roosevelt, their forebears and descendants, the careers of major and minor political figures of the era, the operations of significant presidential boards and commissions, and the history of the U.S. Navy, of Dutchess County and the Hudson Valley region. As a result, researchers have access to Mr. Roosevelt's papers as New York state senator and governor, assistant secretary of the U.S. Navy, and president. They can search the two million pages of Eleanor Roosevelt manuscripts, the papers of Adolf A. Berle, Samuel I. Rosenman and Rexford G. Tugwell, all members of the "brains trust"; the manuscripts of WPA head and wartime advisor Harry L. Hopkins; and the invaluable diaries of Henry Morgenthau, Jr., Secretary of the Treasury and Roosevelt's Dutchess County neighbor. They can wade through the records of the President's Committee on Portal to Portal Travel Time, ponder the records of the War Refugee Board, examine the log of the *Constitution*, and study accounts of activities on board nineteenth-century American whaling ships.

Today, the Library still actively collects materials, following an acquisitions policy centered on the abovementioned categories. Recent additions include the papers of Claude Wickard, the Secretary of Agriculture during World War II, consumer advocate Caroline Ware, Bronx political leader Edward J. Flynn, and Eleanor Roosevelt's friend and biographer Joseph P. Lash. Potential future acquisitions include the papers of Under Secretary of State Sumner

Welles and Associate Supreme Court Justice Robert H. Jackson. Such collections will enable the Library to serve the public even more effectively.

PRIVATE DONORS

Most Library holdings are privately donated historical materials administered under a legal instrument, usually a deed of gift executed by the donor and the National Archives and Records Service. The deed transfers title to the papers to the federal government, empowers the Archivist of the United States to review and close materials that would compromise national security or constitute an unwarranted invasion of personal privacy or result in the defamation of a living person, authorizes the Archivist to dispose of materials of no permanent value or historical interest, and either conveys copyright to the government or retains it for the donor and his or her heirs until a specified future time. The Archivist of the United States delegates the needed authority to implement the provisions of the deed to the Library.

All collections, except the few which the staff has not yet processed, are open for research. Furthermore, less than one percent of the Library's holdings are closed to research under donor restrictions or security classifications. All such security classified materials have been reviewed by the appropriate federal agency, and the donor restricted materials consist of documents that contain information potentially injurious to private citizens. The staff periodically reviews such documents, opening those which no longer require protection. During processing, staff members insert information sheets in folders from which they have removed documents. They will explain to researchers, on request, the procedures for appealing donor restrictions and initiating declassification actions.

PROCESSING COLLECTIONS FOR RESEARCH

When a collection arrives at the Library, an archivist is assigned to process it for research use. This involves reconstructing the original arrangement of the papers or imposing a new arrangement if the original is not discernable, reviewing them for security classified and donor restrictions, performing basic preservation actions such as removing rusty paper clips, flattening documents, rehousing them in acid-free folders and boxes, and preparing a finding aid. The basic finding aid in the Roosevelt Library is the registration statement, a one-page description of each collection in the Library, regardless of size. It includes biographical or administrative data on the person or organization which created the collection, a brief description of the papers, restrictions on access, date span and size, and information on copyright. These statements are available in the Registration Book in the Research Room. Large manuscript collections have detailed finding aids which include the information from the registration statement in expanded form plus a description of series, if needed, or an explanation of file arrangement, and a box-by-box list of folder titles. For several of the more significant or frequently used collections, such as President Roosevelt's Official and Personal Files, the shelf list is alphabetically indexed. Finally, there are subject and surname indices to Eleanor Roosevelt's White House Papers and the diaries of Henry Morgenthau, Jr., both prepared by their respective staffs. In its early years, the Library's archivists began indexing the presidential papers. Although the project was never completed, the Library makes the indices available in the Research Room with the caveat that they cover only a small portion of Mr. Roosevelt's White House files.

Standard processing procedures include the removal of extremely fragile and valuable documents and their replacement with electrostatic copies. In the early 1970s, the diplomatic and cabinet department files of the President's Secretary's File were replaced by copies because the staff correctly anticipated that the volume of research use would be heavy enough to destroy the originals. To date the Library has used electrostatic copying as a preservation device because researchers prefer copies to microfilm and because the Library lacks the manpower and funding to undertake large-scale deacidification and mylar encapsulation. Encapsulation has been reserved for extremely fragile items.

As a general rule, the Library does not open collections for research use until they are completely processed. It will notify individual researchers when a collection becomes available. *Prologue: The Journal of the National Archives* as well as the *American Historical Review* and the *Journal of American History* carry notices of the Roosevelt Library's recent acquisitions and openings of collections for research.

THE LIBRARY'S USERS

The Roosevelt Library, like its sister libraries in the system, is open to all researchers whose research requires the use of its unique resources. Since 1970 it has attracted an average of 300-400 researchers annually who have made 1200 to 1400 research visits. They consist primarily of faculty members, undergraduates, Ph.D. and Master's candidates, journalists and authors. In addition, the Library responds to some 1600 letters a year and roughly 1000 telephone calls. The reference load is handled by a staff of 11 consisting of two supervisory archivists, four archivists, three archives technicians, one photographer, and a machine operator who does the electrostatic copying and microfilming. The archivists and archives technicians serve in the Research Room on a rotating schedule. They provide security, acquaint researchers with Library procedures, and answer questions and telephone calls. Archivists on duty in the Research Room also process collections as time permits.

Library materials may be used only in the Research Room, which is open from 9 a.m. to 4:45 p.m. Monday through Friday, except national holidays. The Library strongly encourages advance inquiry and notice of visit, as it enables the staff to provide researchers with information about the quantity and scope of pertinent materials. The staff will send the researcher an application which may be filled out and returned in advance, a list of the Library's holdings entitled *Historical Materials in the Franklin D. Roosevelt Library*, general information sheets on Library policies and procedures, and on accommodations in the Hyde Park area. Occasionally, there may not be sufficient materials on a topic to warrant a personal visit to the Library, and advance application may save the researcher time and money.

When the researcher arrives at the Library, the archivist has him or her sign the daily register, complete an application, if this has not already been done, and gives the orientation interview. The archivist shows the researcher the location of the finding aids and standard reference works, explains how materials are ordered, and also requests proof of identity. Researchers may bring only essential note-taking materials into the Research Room; storage areas and locked compartments outside the research area are provided for personal belongings. When the researcher has materials to be copied, the archivist will explain the copying procedures. All electrostatic copying is done by a staff member. Personal typewriters and tape recorders are permitted for note-taking purposes. The Library reserves the right to examine any materials brought into the Research Room at the time the researcher leaves.

PREPARATION FOR USING THE COLLECTION

The Library encourages visits by faculty members, professional writers and degree candidates, and while it does not discourage use by undergraduates, and high school and elementary students, it suggests that they follow certain procedures so as to avoid indiscriminate rummaging through manuscript collections. Archivists encourge teachers to have their students work on specific topics and thoroughly familiarize them with the published literature and printed sources so that they will derive the maximum benefit from their visit. Teachers are urged to visit the Library beforehand and, in the case of elementary and high school students, to coordinate their projects and classroom visits with members of the staff. Elementary and secondary teachers who cannot follow these guidelines may arrange for an orientation lecture and film on the Roosevelt period and perhaps a tour of the research facilities, but should not expect free run of the Research Room.

The staff has found over the years that advance preparation, including prior teacher visits, are most beneficial. For almost a decade, now, two teachers and about 15 students on the average from an undergraduate history class at Alma College in Alma, Michigan, have made very successful bi-annual research trips to the Library. The visits last two weeks, and the students complete their research and a draft of their papers before the end of their stay. Our archivists have also worked with several classes of gifted and talented elementary students. Again, advance meetings and/or telephone discussions with teachers about topics and documents have resulted in very profitable student visits.

For the researcher who writes or telephones a request, the archivists try to be as helpful as possible consistent with their other duties and responsibilities. The staff draws a general distinction between reference and research. The former involves consulting Library finding aids and indices to provide guidance, answers to inquiries or general information about pertinent material on particular topics, while the latter refers to a detailed, methodical examination of manuscript files in order to provide answers. Whereas the staff is ever ready to undertake reference work, it generally does not engage in extensive detailed research in files. This is true for several reasons. The staff is not large enough to handle such tasks and must husband its time and resources. More important, it does not presume to have the expertise that the researcher has, nor can it make judgments about another's research. In the final analysis, the archivists always encourage researchers engaged in major projects, including dissertations, articles, and books, to visit the Library and do their own research, or, if that is impossible, to hire a professional researcher. Only the researcher who has examined the files in person can be certain of seeing everything on his or her topic.

Of course, the staff does handle inquiries for specific and easily discoverable information and documents. The most frequent concern the activities and opinions of the President and Mrs. Roosevelt. Requests for sources of statements attributed to them are very common. In responding to inquiries, the archivists check published sources, finding aids, old reference letters, and readily identifiable files in manuscript collections. The staff maintains an information file to assist it in responding to frequently asked questions about the Roosevelts, and some archivists index their correspondence to facilitate answering inquiries. The archivists generally devote four hours to an inquiry. Inquiries that require a search of a manuscript file must be accompanied by reasonably precise data on the addressor and addressee of a letter or the wording of a quotation. The chances of locating vaguely identified, undated documents or statements are very slim. In cases where researchers need extensive documentary material but cannot visit the Library or retain the services of a professional researcher, the staff will provide copies of entire manuscript files, rather than examining each potentially valuable file. The Library will provide a list of professional researchers in the local area whom researchers can hire to do their research.

The Library makes finding aids available either in electrostatic copies for a fee or through inter-library loan. The Library's finding aids have recently been copied for inclusion in the *National Inventory of Documentary Sources in the United States*, a microfiche publication compiled by Chadwyck-Healy, Inc.

NOT ONLY MANUSCRIPTS

In addition to manuscripts, the Library has a variety of other resources available to aid the researcher. There is the book collection of 44,500 volumes built around President Roosevelt's personal library of 15,000 books and pamphlets. From boyhood Roosevelt collected books on history, economics, government, public affairs, and travel. Also housed in the Library are his special collections of books on the history of the U.S. Navy, of Dutchess County, British and American literary classics, early juveniles, and ornithology. The printed materials holdings serve mainly as resources for staff in dealing with research inquiries and for researchers working at the Library.

The Library has acquired and provides reference service for some 100,000 photographs, 700 reels of motion picture film, and sound recordings of almost all known speeches of President Roosevelt and a large selection of those of Mrs. Roosevelt. The photograph collection is arranged both alphabetically by subject, with separate headings for Franklin and Eleanor Roosevelt, and by individual collections. Most individual collections will eventually be integrated into the subject file. There is a card index, arranged chronologically and by subject for the FDR photographs, and a chronological index, with a subject index planned, for Eleanor Roosevelt's pictures. The Library makes black and white prints and negatives in its own laboratory; all color processing is sent to commercial laboratories. The staff will search for individual photographs, if sufficiently identified, and will select prints for research projects and provide electrostatic copies for selection purposes. As with manuscript research, the archivists encourage researchers to visit the Library and do their own research. The staff advises researchers to purchase electrostatic copies of photographs for the initial stages of their work, since this saves laboratory processing time and may also cut costs overall.

The staff has prepared a card index to the sound recordings collection as well as special lists of the speeches and other utterances of Franklin and Eleanor Roosevelt, and can provide reel to reel and cassette dubbings. There is also a card index to the collection of newsreels on the Roosevelt presidency, the documentaries, and home movies, and a detailed description of the newsreels is being prepared. There are 16mm reference prints and/or 3/4-inch videocassettes of all films available for viewing at the Library. The Library cannot duplicate films or videocassettes, but relies on the National Archives for such assistance. Audio recordings and films are not loaned, except under unusual circumstances, and then only for reference use. The Library refers to private film libraries or the National Audiovisual Center all persons seeking to borrow documentary films on the Roosevelts, the New Deal, and World War II for public showing.

As part of reference service, the staff guides researchers to sources on their topics in other repositories, and provides what assistance it can with the thorny problem of copyright. The archivists do not consider themselves copyright lawyers. They will provide as much specific information as possible on the holdings of the Library, including the names and addresses of copyright holders. *Historical Materials in the Franklin D. Roosevelt Library*, the Library's information sheets, and the introduction to the Registration Book contain general statements about the new copyright law. If researchers have specific legal problems relating to interpretation of the law, the staff will recommend that they contact a copyright lawyer or their publisher. In general, anything written by President Roosevelt is in the public domain. Although the writings of public officials in their official capacities are also considered to be in the public domain, researchers are encouraged to consult copyright holders in every doubtful case.

PUBLICATIONS AND PUBLIC EDUCATION PROGRAMS

The Library engages in a publications program to make its holdings more widely known and available. Its most widespread publication is *Historical Materials in the Franklin D. Roosevelt Library*, which is updated periodically to include new acquisitions. In addition, the staff has edited various documentary publications in letterpress and microfilm. The former include *Franklin D. Roosevelt and Conservation 1910-1945* (2 volumes) and *Franklin D. Roosevelt and Foreign Affairs 1933-1937* (3 volumes). Microfilm publications include the *Correspondence of Franklin D. Roosevelt and Winston Churchill 1939-45* (6 rolls), the *Diaries of Adolf A. Berle* (3 rolls), the *Press Conferences of Franklin D. Roosevelt* (13 rolls), the *Papers of Henry A. Wallace* (54 rolls), and, most recently, *Franklin D. Roosevelt and Foreign Affairs 1937-August 1939* (5 rolls). The microfilm edition of *Franklin D. Roosevelt and Foreign Affairs* has appeared in facsimile letterpress editions published by Clearwater and Garland Presses in New York. To give researchers a better grasp of what has been published about Franklin D. Roosevelt and his times, the Library has compiled and annotated a bibliography entitled *The Era of Franklin D. Roosevelt: A Bibliography of Selected Periodical, Dissertation, and Essay Literature, 1945-1971*.

A supplement to the bibliography, covering the years 1972 to 1980, is nearly completed.

The staff also engages in some forms of public education as part of its reference duties. Archivists provide guided tours of the research and stack areas, by appointment. Prior to the tours, there is usually an orientation lecture on the history and operations of the Library, and groups may also arrange to see films on the Roosevelts and their times. Due to small staff size, the need to concentrate on the reference and processing, and the general appeal of the Library research program to faculty and graduate students, the Library has not been involved extensively in outreach programs. However, the Library has assisted the Hyde Park School system in creating an educational packet on Franklin D. Roosevelt for junior high school students to help fulfill the New York State local history requirement. Also, the Director of the Library speaks to public groups in the area and at conferences. The Library has co-sponsored conferences on Franklin D. Roosevelt and hosted the International Conference on Archives, a conference on youth sponsored by the Eleanor Roosevelt Institute, and a conference on peace and human rights sponsored by Arm and Hammer.

Although the Library does not make inter-library loans of documents, except for some material on microfilm, it does loan documents for exhibit purposes. Such loans are made under very strict conditions. The documents themselves must be in good physical condition or they will not be loaned. The borrowing institution must provide proper security, house the documents under appropriate temperature and humidity, and follow the Library's prescriptions on lighting, to name a few conditions. Institutions which cannot meet such requirements will not be loaned original materials, but can purchase and display electrostatic or photographic copies.

Since the Library has only recently acquired a computer, it is not possible to gauge its impact on the archival program. The first application of the computer will be for administrative matters. Since this will include statistical record keeping, it will affect the archives because it maintains detailed statistics on the volume of holdings, the number of written and oral inquiries, the number of items served, and of course, the number of researchers and annual research visits. The staff intends to apply the computer to storage and retrieval of reference letters on recurring topics in order to speed up and simplify reference work. Computer software will eventually assist in the creation and indexing of finding aids.

A MATURE LIBRARY

After nearly 45 years of operation, the Roosevelt Library is entitled to be considered a "mature" library. It has acquired most of the major collections from the Roosevelt era that it is likely to receive, has processed nearly all of them, and its number of researchers has held steady for the past ten years. The fact is, however, that the Library is still accessioning materials, still processing and beginning to reprocess collections, and still drawing large numbers of researchers annually. During the drafting of this paper, the Joseph P. Lash papers arrived. And lest it be thought that the Library's collecting days will end when the papers of the last Roosevelt administration stalwart pass through its doors, it should be remembered that Mr. Roosevelt took much interest in local history. In pursuit of that interest, the Library has acquired in the past five years the papers of the Hudson River Conservation Society and Scenic Hudson materials relating to the Storm King controversy. The staff recently finished refoldering and reboxing the President's Official File in acid-free materials and has begun the same process for the President's Personal File.

Certainly the centennial celebrations for Franklin D. Roosevelt (1982) and Eleanor Roosevelt (1984) have stimulated research interest. But the fact remains that interest in the Roosevelt era remains high and will remain high simply because of the great events—a major depression and a world war—which it encompasses. As late as November of last year, the Library was still averaging about three research visits a day, and this during what is supposed to be its slow season! The supplement to *The Era of Franklin D. Roosevelt* will contain over 2800 entries—a concrete testimony to the continuing study of the Roosevelt period and proof that the Roosevelt Library's future as a research institution is bright and lively.

Reference and Research in Regional History Centers

Glen A. Gildemeister

Most of the archives and manuscript repositories in the United States fall into one of five broad categories: federal repositories, state archives, private manuscript libraries, corporate (profit and non-profit) archives, and college or university archives. Regional history research centers, a recent arrival on the archives scene, are a hybrid incorporating some aspect of all of the above categories. Although they comprise only a small portion of the archives field these regional centers have multiplied rapidly in the last two decades and the resources they now offer researchers are substantial.[1]

REGIONAL HISTORY CENTERS: AN INTRODUCTION

The proliferation of regional centers over the past two decades rests on a number of pillars. Such phenomena as the Bicentennial Celebration, the rise of historic site preservation at the local level, and the use of history in popular television mini-series have built a growing public constituency which supports and uses historical research centers. The federal government significantly increased its support to new ideas in historic preservation in the 1960s and 1970s through the National Endowment for the Humanities, the National Historic Publications and Records Commission, the National Trust for Historic Preservation, and even the National Park Service. Universities created a number of regional centers in an attempt to mitigate the disastrous effects of the passing of the World War II baby boom through their gates. Such centers attracted potential students, provided jobs for unemployed graduates in history, often brought in grant monies, and helped build a constituency for the

---

Mr. Gildemeister is Director of the Earl W. Hayter Regional History Center, Northern Illinois University, DeKalb, Illinois 60115.

© 1986 by The Haworth Press, Inc. All rights reserved.

school. Most importantly, the social turbulence of the 1960s created new fields of research as black people, women, Hispanics, blue collar workers, and ethnic enclaves began to seek historical antecedence and validation for their civil rights campaigns, cultural traditions, social values, and distinctive identities in the American milieu.

The activism of the 1960s has abated, the federal government has cut back on support, and enrollments have continued to decline, but the regional centers have grown and flourished. They fill a void between overburdened state historical agencies and the local library or museum which cannot divert resources to extensive archives programs. They offer a place where small businesses, local organizations, families, churches, and local governments can preserve their records and still have access to them. Proximity to both donors and researchers—compared to an often distant state library—has brought strong growth in acquisitions and use. Thus regional history centers are fast becoming the repository of first resort for people involved in historic building preservation, local and family history research, and oral history projects.

REGIONAL CENTERS
AND THE NEW SOCIAL HISTORY

What distinguishes regional centers from their more traditional counterparts in the archives field? The characteristics peculiar to regional centers are worth noting since they require reference services which differ somewhat from a corporate archives or a private manuscript repository. First, these centers strongly emphasize collections development in the "new social history": families, immigrants, farmers, the working class, women, poverty, social welfare, and popular culture. Second, these centers are usually a small part of a larger institution—often a university—and thus have a dual responsibility for the parent institution's records as well as private manuscript or records collections. Third, the scope of their mission in collecting and service is regional, with the region defined by a combination of geography, political boundaries, economic activity, and the service area of the parent institution. Fourth, many of these centers hold both private and public records in equal measure. Finally, many regional history research centers are members of state archives networks.

The Earl W. Hayter Regional History Center at Northern Illinois

University is typical of most regional centers. Its collecting and public service area is that of the university, the northern tier of eighteen counties in Illinois. The region extends from Lake Michigan on the east to the Mississippi River on the west and from the Wisconsin border on the north to the Illinois River Valley on the south. It is a region with a commercial, political, ethnic, and agricultural history distinct from surrounding areas. Within this region the Hayter Center actively collects public (local government) records and private records collections from businesses, churches, farms, labor unions, politicians, and civic or social organizations. It also has responsibility for collecting and preserving Northern Illinois University's records. Thus the Center has three distinct sets of collections: University Archives, Local Government Records, Regional Manuscript Collections. Each is maintained separately both physically on the shelves and intellectually in the finding aids. Guides, checklists, inventories, and indices provide reference access to the file folder, volume, or item level. The Center also offers researchers a general bound reference collection of archival directories and guides, county histories and atlases, and basic genealogical research materials.[2]

ACCESSING THE CENTER HOLDINGS

The Center provides researchers a variety of finding aids to access its holdings. The Local Government Records collection is part of a six university statewide network created by the Illinois State Archives called the Illinois Regional Archives Depository system, or I.R.A.D. The State Archives has published a guide which allows access to all records series held in the I.R.A.D. system throughout the state.[3] Two hundred fifty typescript inventories complement this guide and give detailed information about each series the Center holds. An unpublished guide gives subject access to the Center's 180 Regional Manuscript Collections: a typescript inventory for each collection gives detailed access to the file level. An automated data base maintained on the Center's computer directs researchers using the University Archives to one of forty-six records series inventories. Finally, specialized checklists and item level indices to photographs, newspapers, posters, artifacts, drawings, films, and reference works complete the array of finding aids. In sum, three major guides—one for each area—lead the researcher to the Center's 475 collection or series inventories.[4] The inventories follow a standard archival format and give the researcher provenance information, a description on record quantity and format, a historical or biographical sketch, a scope and content note, and a container listing to the volume or file folder level (see Figure 1).

FIGURE 1

Accession 1/238/7   Sheet 1 of 1

Series _____   **I R A D**   Date prepared 1/12/83
                                                                received _____
Location microfilm   returned _____
                                DESCRIPTIVE INVENTORY   revised _____
                                                                received _____
                                                                 filed _____
                                                             Intern RJS

1. County LaSalle
   a. City _____
   b. Township _____
   c. Other _____

2. Office Circuit Clerk

3. Function To serve as a permanent record of Naturalization proceedings
   _____

4. Title Naturalization Records _____

5. Labeling none

6. Dates December 1876 – September 1906

7. Quantity   vols. _____ l.f. _____ cu. ft. _____ folders _____ film reels 3

8. Indexing An index is included at the beginning of each reel

9. Arrangement chronological

10. HRS Citation LaSalle County card 2 24156, card 3 24158

11. Contents This series contains the Declaration of Intention to become a citizen.
    That record includes the applicant's name, nativity, place and length of residence,
    date of enlistment, name of presiding judge, an oath affirming loyalty to the
    principles and constitution of the United States as well as renouncing allegiance
    to the former sovereign; the signature of the applicant, certification and signature
    of the county clerk and the date of the petition.
    _____

12. Other Information For LaSalle County Naturalization Records, 1840-1876, see I.R.A.D.
    inventory 236/1.

AR D-73.1A

The Center has a small staff—three faculty, four graduate assistants, one clerk—and all get involved in reference work. The reading room receptionist and the manuscripts curator have primary responsibility for reading room reference with graduate assistants handling mail queries and genealogical searches. Each of the three major areas of collections demands reference services which, while similar, differ because of the constituency using the records. Much of the reference work in the public records is a search for a specific bit of information rather than general historical research on a topic. Genealogical search requests by mail account for over eighty percent of the use of the local government records and these come in from across the country. The Center, like most archives, will provide answers to specific genealogical requests. Do you have a marriage record for James and Mary Reilly from Carroll County, December 15, 1847? Can you provide copies of naturalization papers for Joseph Stachowicz from LaSalle County in 1846 or 1847? Graduate assistants conduct the search and reply by return mail including a photocopy of the document if available.

Telephone requests for specific documents come in from county administrators (clerks, judges, coroners, sheriffs, recorders) who need a record or file to conduct current business. Do you have Kane County Circuit Court Case No. 8327 from 1933 litigation between the City of Aurora and the Burlington Railroad? University administrators also phone in requests for a particular past budget, class schedule, photograph, or student record. Combined, these mail and telephone administrative or genealogical requests account for about twenty percent of the total reference services provided. Center staff answer these questions by return call or letter at no charge, usually within an hour. This service strengthens the Center's utility within the parent institution, links the university with the public, affords records management to local officials, and complements the Center's public service in the preservation of the documentary heritage of the region.

Genealogical and administrative reference accounts for only twenty percent of all reference work; the other eighty percent is providing primary sources for patrons researching the history of the region's towns, farms, churches, buildings, railroads, social customs, businesses, churches, immigrants, and the history of the university itself. About half of the researchers who come into the Center's reading room are affiliated with the university and half are from off campus. The broad range of researchers has implications for reference work. University faculty and graduate students generally have strong research skills and some experience in using archives; many of those coming in from off campus have never been in an archives before.[5] They learn of the Center's holdings through public exhibits, promotional articles in regional mass media, accession notices published in journals, national archives guides and directories, the National Union Catalog of Manuscript Collections, or through word of mouth from donors or other researchers.[6]

THE REFERENCE PROCESS

In the Center's reading room, the reference process begins with the first contact between the researcher and a Center staff member since the stacks are closed and registration is required. Researchers working in the Center must complete a registration form on the first visit and sign in on a daily log for subsequent visits. (See Figure 2.) Registration informs the researcher of Center policy on the use of the materials and affords the opportunity for an entrance interview with a staff member. This interview, while brief and informal, is the linchpin to good reference service. The interview establishes the relationship between the researcher and the reference staff which underwrites effective reference service. A successful interview will lay out the groundrules for using the collections, explain the finding aids, make clear the services which will and will not be provided, elicit the nature and scope of research interest, and conclude with suggestions for starting research in the finding aids. Registration also allows the Center to accumulate use statistics, provides for the security of its holdings, assists in formulating collections development policy, and allows the researchers an opportunity to become aware of others working on similar projects.

Most researchers coming into the Center have fairly simple requests which the reading room attendant can fulfill; the manuscripts curator handles more complex and difficult research projects. Reference personnel in regional centers face the same problems as their colleagues in more traditional archives. Where does reference end and research begin? How does a small staff deal with the heterogeneity of research interests? What is the right balance between document preservation/security and fair, open access to the past? How can both researcher's and donor's rights be protected? Difficult problems such as these occur daily and can be solved only on a case by case basis using traditional archival practice, common

FIGURE 2

EARL W. HAYTER REGIONAL HISTORY CENTER
NORTHERN ILLINOIS UNIVERSITY

Research Policy for Use of Collections

1. All new researchers are required to fill out a Researcher Registration Form. (See other side)

2. Briefcases, portfolios, and coats should be checked with the reading room attendant.

3. Pencils and ballpoints <u>only</u> are permitted; they can be obtained from the reading room attendant if necessary. No marking of or writing on archival materials is allowed, and annotations found in the materials should not be removed.

4. All materials are to be used in the designated research area only. Do not write on, alter, fold anew, trace, or handle materials in any way likely to damage them.

5. Use only one box at a time. Remove one folder at a time. Do not remove items from folders or alter the order and arrangement of the material.

6. No smoking, food, or beverages allowed when using the research area.

7. Photoduplication of non-restricted items is permitted. Please check with the reading room attendant; he/she will do the copying. The charge is 15¢ per page.

8. It is the responsibility of the researcher to secure permission to publish material from the Earl W. Hayter Regional History Center. The researcher also assumes all responsibility for possible infringement of copyright and/or literary property rights in the act of copying or in the subsequent use of materials.

9. In citing the materials, please use the full name of the collections or material used and the Earl W. Hayter Regional History Center. For example: Letter from John Roberts to Isaac Rhys, January 6, 1978, John Roberts Papers, Box 6, Folder 3, held by the Earl W. Hayter Regional History Center, Northern Illinois University.

10. Please report any errors or discrepancies found in using the collections to the reading room attendant.

I have read and agree to comply with the above use policy.

Signature   Date

sense, personal experience, and, of course, legal applications concerning access, privacy, and copyright.[7] The goal is to provide equal and fair service in all cases and to strike a balance when interests conflict. A careful registration which explains use policies and opens the finding aids to the researcher best accomplishes this goal.

Once the researcher has access to the guides and inventories she is free to request any materials open to the public and a page will bring the materials to the reading room.[8] Reference service from that point forward consists only of answering questions and providing copy services. Since the Center strongly discourages donors from restricting access to collections, less than one percent of the Center's holdings are not open to the public. Public access to restricted records is possible only if the researcher has written permission from the donor or a legal right to see the record. A more serious reference problem is the reproduction of documents by xerography. Reference staff will copy documents for patrons at a cost of fifteen cents per page but can refuse this service if copying will either damage the document or violate copyright law. The Center also provides reasonable numbers of copies at no charge to donors, to university officials, and to answer genealogical search letters. Micrographic and photographic copy services are available on a flat fee per roll or print through the university's reprographic department.

As is true with most repositories, the collections do not circulate nor are they available on interlibrary loan. There are several exceptions to this policy. Donors of private manuscript collections may borrow from their collections for a short period of time and university officials may sign out records from their own departments for three weeks. Local government records on microfilm are available on interlibrary loan through the Illinois State Archives for use at any one of the six depositories across the state.

Although the Center does not conduct an exit interview as standard reference policy the registration form does provide for some of the information which is usually included in an exit interview. Advice to researchers regarding citations, permission to publish, and copyright is given on this form and the reference staff keeps a written record of what materials are used for future reference. Through the registration process the Center can determine how many people are using the collections, who they are, where they come from, and what they are using. A corollary benefit accrues when researchers return and cannot remember what they have and have not researched. A simple telephone log of queries answered, a mail reference file, and the daily sign in sheets complete the reference statistical picture. Taken together these data give a detailed user profile, a measure of reference success, and a means to chart reference growth over time. Such data are used for institutional reporting, reshaping collections development, targeting outreach programs, and producing checklists of materials in popular subjects. Researchers engaged in substantial projects are asked to provide the Center with a copy of the finished paper or publication.

NOTES

1. There are approximately fifty such centers around the United States with the greatest concentration in the upper Midwest. The best available introduction to regional history research centers is a special issue of the *Midwestern Archivist* VI, No. 2, 1982, which surveys the state networks to which most of the midwest centers belong. For a detailed look at the scholarly premises which undergird a regional approach to historical research, see Glenn Porter, editor, *Regional Economic History: the Mid-Atlantic Area Since 1700*. Wilmington, Delaware: Eleutherian Mills-Hagley Foundation, 1976.

2. The bound reference collection contains fewer than 3,000 volumes but it is heavily used. Researchers find the local, county, and family histories a good starting point and use archival guides and directories to continue research beyond the Center.

3. Roy C. Turnbaugh, Jr. *A Guide to County Records in the Illinois Regional Archives*. Springfield: Illinois State Archives, 1983.

4. The Center employs an amalgam of complementary but distinct finding aids instead of a single unified catalog or data base for several reasons. First, the three collections are unique in origin, content, arrangement, and development. Second, each area has a distinct set of users and a researcher rarely uses materials from all three types of records. Third, the Center does not hold title to or control description of the local government records: by state statute these belong to the State Archives.

5. A study based on registrations from 1979 to 1894 yielded the following profile: male, 53%; female, 47%; university affiliated, 56%; non-university, 44%; local area, 12%; other Illinois, 27%; out of state, 5%. Collection use analysis showed 45% using primarily the University Archives; 34%, the Regional Manuscript Collections; 15%, the reference collections only; and 6%, the I.R.A.D. collection.

6. Notes on new accessions are regularly sent to appropriate state and national journals such as local genealogical or historical society newsletters. Exceptional collections or those with national significance are reported to the National Union Catalog of Manuscript Collections and the Center is listed in all major national archives directories.

7. For a succinct discussion of privacy, access, and copyright see Sue E. Holbert, *Archives and Manuscripts: Reference and Access*. Chicago: Society of American Archivists, 1977, pp. 5-6, 16-18. On the issue of copyright in unpublished materials the Center's Deed of Gift dedicates such literary rights as the donor may possess in the materials to the public domain. Further, "the researcher also assumes all responsibility for possible infringement of copyright" in using the materials when he signs the registration form.

8. The question of where reference ends and research begins is perhaps the most vexing of all reference judgements. The Center takes a conservative approach and agrees with Kenneth Duckett's advice that "it must be the researcher's responsibility to seek out and use the manuscripts necessary for his research." *Modern Manuscripts: A Practical Manual for Their Management, Care, and Use*. Nashville: American Association for State and Local History, 1975, p. 236.

SOURCES

Bordin, Ruth B., and Warner, Robert M. *The Modern Manuscript Library*. New York and London: The Scarecrow Press, Inc., 1966.

Duckett, Kenneth W. *Modern Manuscripts: A Practical Manual for Their Management and Use*. Nashville: American Association for State and Local History, 1975.

Holbert, Sue E. *Archives and Manuscripts: Reference and Access*. Chicago: Society of American Archivists, 1977.

Jones, Houston G. *Local Government Records: An Introduction to Their Management, Preservation, and Use*. Nashville: American Association for State and Local History, 1980.

Schellenberg, T. R. *The Management of Archives*. New York and London: Columbia University Press, 1965.

Expanded Access to Archival Sources

Thomas Hickerson

Providing users of historical records with effective access to the wealth of documentation housed in archives and manuscript repositories is a fundamental goal of archival practice. Meeting this objective has never been easy, and the continuing growth in the number of repositories and the size of their holdings has increased the difficulties. This task has been made more complex by expansion in the number and variety of uses of archival holdings. The broadened scope of historical investigation, including use by social scientists, genealogists, and journalists, has increased the need for common access points to different types of documentation housed in a variety of repositories. While this need for multi-institutional access has grown in recent years, it is not a new concern of users of historical records.

Clearly stating this long sought ideal, the historian and educator, Theodore C. Blegen, wrote in 1947:

> I have mentioned a master key. By that I mean a great inventory of archives and manuscripts, a key that will open closed doors—in fact, doors that many of us do not even know exist. We need some way of really knowing what has been preserved out of the past in the hundreds of collections throughout the land.
>
> I do not know what form it will take. Perhaps it will be an index to a thousand guides prepared after the best models we have been able to devise; perhaps it will be a master union guide. Certainly it will be a flexible scheme, controlling what has been done in amassing historical treasures and keeping abreast of current growth.[1]

Mr. Hickerson is Chairman of the Department of Manuscripts and University Archives at Cornell University, Ithaca, NY 14853. He is author of many works on the automation of archives.

© 1986 by The Haworth Press, Inc. All rights reserved.

It is unlikely that Theodore Blegen envisioned the development of online computer networks, accessible nationwide, disseminating up-to-date bibliographic information regarding archives and manuscript resources. And while exhaustive comprehensiveness and universal accessibility are still beyond our practical expectations, substantial progress has been made in the development of the capacity to provide the kind of integrated, multi-institutional access of which Blegen dreamed.

Success in the effort to broaden access to information regarding archival holdings has come slowly. In briefly describing the progress that has been made since the time of Blegen's plea, this article shows some of the difficulties of generating adequate financial resources and maintaining sufficient institutional commitment and cooperation. However, at the same time, it also attempts to convey a sense of the strong concern which archivists have consistently felt regarding this issue.

In describing the accomplishments of the last few years, particular attention is given to the design and development of the archival control enhancements to the Research Libraries Information Network (RLIN), the automated information system of the Research Libraries Group (RLG). The development of the RLIN Archives and Manuscripts Control system was integral to the process for the compilation and implementation of the revised USMARC Format for Archival and Manuscripts Control,[2] and the cooperative nature of system design and implementation does, in many ways, epitomize current aims and opportunities.

Expanded access will affect the provision of reference services by archivists and librarians. It will be several years before we can assess the overall effect of current developments. Yet, by examining these new capabilities, archivists and librarians will be able to prepare for and take advantage of these opportunities.

A NATIONAL REGISTER OF HISTORICAL MANUSCRIPTS

In 1946, the American Historical Association (AHA) established a Committee on Manuscripts, chaired by Herbert A. Kellar.[3] This committee prepared a plan for compiling a union catalog of manuscripts, including staffing and budgetary projections, and recommended that the Association seek foundation support to fund the compilation. This plan was not adopted, however, and in 1948,

AHA chose to discontinue their Committee on Manuscripts, suggesting that the Society of American Archivists (SAA) and the American Association for State and Local History (AASLH) form a committee to address the issue.[4]

SAA and AASLH accepted the challenge and, in 1949, formed a Joint Committee on Historical Manuscripts, chaired by Lester J. Cappon and including a representative of the Library of Congress (LC). In 1951, this committee endorsed the concept of a national guide to historical manuscripts, comparable to the Library of Congress's National Union Catalog for books, and the committee began to search for an institution willing and able to serve as the headquarters. However, in the fall of 1951, LC proposed that a national register be established at the Library as a subsidiary of the National Union Catalog. It was proposed that, after the formulation of uniform rules for the cataloging of manuscript collections, LC would print cards for its own collections and would edit and print cards from copy submitted by other repositories. Copies of these cards would be made available at a small cost to repositories for their own use, and it was suggested that LC might print a book catalog of all cards received in the preceding year and offer it for sale at a reasonable price.[5] It is unlikely that it is a mere coincidence that the Librarian of Congress who approved this offer was Luther H. Evans, the organizer and first director of the Works Progress Administration's Historical Records Survey, the first major survey of America's documentary resources.

By the spring of 1954, after considerable professional review, a widely acceptable set of rules for the cataloging of manuscript collections had been compiled.[6] However, further progress was delayed until 1958, when the Library received a $200,000 grant from the Council on Library Resources, Inc. to support the project. The first card in the series was printed in June 1959, and the first volume of the *National Union Catalog of Manuscript Collections* (NUCMC) was published in 1962. In establishing the scope of the Catalog, four basic guidelines were adopted:

1. only collections, rather than single manuscripts, are to be reported;
2. collections must be located in a public or quasi-public repository that regularly admits researchers;
3. institutional or governmental archives are to be excluded if they are being maintained by the originating agency;

4. collections consisting entirely of photocopies and transcripts are generally excluded.[7]

Although interpreted and applied liberally, these original guidelines still govern inclusion. With the publication of its twentieth issue in 1983, NUCMC has published descriptions of some 50,740 collections located in 1,241 different repositories and has indexed them by approximately 538,000 references to topical subjects and personal, family, corporate, and geographic names.[8]

Thousands of scholars, archivists, librarians, and genealogists will attest to the valuable role that NUCMC has played during the last two decades; yet, it has not met objectives envisioned for a national register. The reasons for this are highly relevant to current efforts to expand bibliographic access and involve the scope, methodology, and nature of participation in NUCMC. Not including institutional or governmental archives was an important limitation at the time of NUCMC's inception. During the last two decades, the broadened scope of historical research, the remarkable growth in the number of university, church, and corporate archives, and the dramatic increase in the size of the holdings of state and federal repositories have combined to substantially heighten the significance of this exclusion. The general descriptions of repository holdings which appeared in Hamer's *Guide to Archives and Manuscripts in the United States* (1961)[9] and in the National Historical Publications and Records Commission's (NHPRC) *Directory of Archives and Manuscripts in the United States* (1978)[10] have provided valuable information regarding archives holdings, but neither provides the integration and specificity necessary to meet current access needs.

That NUCMC's bibliographic data is not in machine-readable form significantly limits the techniques available for producing the Catalog. Automated production was not feasible in NUCMC's early years, nor did manual compilation restrict its usefulness. However, as the difficulties inherent in the use of numerous volumes and multiple indexes have grown, the benefits to be derived from electronic processing and dissemination of bibliographic information have expanded. This limitation affects both the currency of information and the nature of participation. The inability to update information or remove outdated or inaccurate descriptions often leads repositories to delay reporting until all probable additions to a collection have arrived and until detailed arrangement and description have been completed. Since this delay may be lengthy, repositories often view reporting to NUCMC as an independent function rather than as an integral part of repository procedures for providing control and access.

That the long-term costs of expanding bibliographic access will largely fall on archival programs and their parent institutions is evident. Experience suggests that neither end users, nor the federal government on their behalf, will support the costs of maintaining a national data base. In order for repositories to consistently allocate resources necessary to support this activity, it must be integral to those processes necessary to meet basic repository goals.

NATIONAL INFORMATION SYSTEMS

The remarkable growth of automated capabilities for the processing, storing, and transmitting of data has dramatically increased the opportunities for the sharing of archival information. Although archivists' initial uses of computer assistance were for the production of detailed indexes, the generation of compatible data for inter-institutional exchange and the development of a national data base were primary concerns from the first.[11] These concerns took on a concrete form when the staff of the NHPRC decided in 1976 to expand their data base of general repository descriptions to include bibliographic information regarding archives and manuscript collections.[12] When in 1977, the NHPRC requested that the Council of the Society of American Archivists endorse its effort, the Council responded by directing the formation of a National Information Systems Task Force (NISTF), chaired by Richard H. Lytle of the Smithsonian Institution, to examine the existing efforts to develop national information systems and to anticipate the role of the Society in this process.[13]

By 1981, the members of NISTF had come to the conclusion that the role of SAA was to develop and maintain standards which would make feasible the inter-institutional exchange of information rather than to build or operate an information system. A study conducted by Elaine D. Engst (Cornell University) in the summer of 1980 had concluded that various types of repositories have similar needs and responsiblities to provide physical and intellectual control of and access to their holdings, and that commonly accepted methods of archival description are used to carry out these functions.[14] However, despite the use of common methods and informational elements by repositories, it was clear that efforts to develop viable information-sharing mechanisms would be obstructed by the lack of a common nomenclature for recording information. Therefore, NISTF initiated the development of a data element dictionary and an exchange format.

NISTF established a Working Group, chaired by David Bearman (NISTF Project Director) and composed of representatives of the National Archives and Records Service, the Library of Congress, the Research Libraries Group, and the NHPRC Data Base participants. A preliminary data element dictionary prepared by this Working Group was issued for professional review in February 1982. This dictionary was intended to provide standard definitions for all information elements employed in any and all archives, record centers, and manuscript repositories.

The compilation of a comprehensive data element dictionary was necessary to the development of an exchange format. It was essential that the format contain specified fields for all data elements required for archival management, including administrative data as well as bibliographic information. It was also important that the format conform to appropriate national and international standards for exchange of bibliographic information in machine-readable form. The most widely used standard for exchange of bibliographic data is the USMARC format. However, the MARC format for manuscripts, published in 1973,[15] was primarily designed for the cataloging of individual items and had been widely repudiated by archivists. Fortunately, LC indicated that it was willing to make substantial revisions and to allow SAA to conduct the revision process.

In the fall of 1982, the data element dictionary and the exchange format were accepted by SAA Council. In January of 1983, the format was approved by the American Library Association (ALA) Committee on the Representation in Machine-Readable Form of Bibliographic Information (MARBI), and was published by LC in late 1984. This format does embody the collection approach to cataloging and includes all data elements listed in the dictionary. As a result of discussions with the Standards Committee of the ALA Division on Rare Books and Manuscripts, fields particularly appropriate for the cataloging of publications handwritten before the advent of printing were added. In addition, those fields which allow the format to be used for single item cataloging and those fields essential to the processing requirements of existing bibliographic systems were retained. These inclusions broaden the acceptability and usability of the format and are consistent with NISTF's desire to meet the needs of all types of repositories. They are also consistent with the diverse nature of archival holdings, making it possible for repositories to describe within a single format all the various types of archives and manuscript material that they hold.[16]

RLIN ARCHIVES AND MANUSCRIPT CONTROL (AMC)

In early 1981, while NISTF was beginning the development of a format to allow the standardized recording and exchange of archival information, a project was initiated at Yale University by Lawrence Dowler to develop an automated system to process and transmit that information nationally. With funding from the U.S. Office of Education's Title II-C (Research Libraries) Program, this project sought to compile a functional requirements statement for developing enhancements to RLIN specifically designed for the machine-readable cataloging of archives and manuscripts.

RLIN is principally the integrated technical processing system of the Research Libraries Group, supporting bibliographic searching, acquisitions, cataloging, interlibrary loan, and, as of January 1984, archives and manuscripts control.[17] Within the bibliographic data base, there are seven major files, based on format of materials: Books, Films, Maps, Sound Recordings, Scores, Serials, and Archival Control. Searches of the data base can be limited to a single file or extended through all files. While the system provides certain format-specific features, the basic processing functions are the same for all files. RLIN also includes an online Authorities file and four specialized data bases.

RLG is a consortium, founded in 1974, which provides a system of software, hardware, cooperative agreements, and coordinated procedures that are designed to enable libraries to meet their commitments to collect, organize, preserve, and provide access to information necessary for education, research, and scholarship. The partnership currently includes some sixty owner, associate, and special members. Comprised predominately of research libraries, the membership also includes special libraries, museums, and state archival programs.

RLG staff were quite excited by the possibilities which the project offered and formed a Task Force on Special Formats to assist the staff at Yale. Chaired by Barbara Brown of RLG and supported by funds from the National Endowment for the Humanities (NEH), this Task Force included archivists from a broad range of institutions, to ensure that the system design would meet the needs of a wide range of repositories. The functional requirements report, compiled by Lofton Abrams and Suzanne Lengyel of the Yale Library, was completed in February 1982, and the initial design work was begun by RLG staff in the fall of 1982.

With the awarding of additional Office of Education, Title II-C funds ($400,000 for 1983 and $425,000 for 1984), a joint project of Yale, Cornell, and Stanford University Libraries, the Hoover Institution, and RLG was initiated in January 1983. The primary goals of the project have been:

1. the design, development, and implementation of enhancements to RLIN to facilitate the accessioning, cataloging, and management of archives and manuscript holdings;
2. the cooperative development of cataloging procedures, conventions, and standards based on the USMARC Format for Archival and Manuscripts Control and compatible with the RLIN technical processing system and the integrated data base;
3. compilation of bibliographic information and comprehensive cataloging of the holdings of participating institutions.[18]

During 1983, project staff from participating repositories were directly involved in the design and implementation process. At a meeting held at RLG headquarters in Stanford, California in March, project staff reviewed the design specifications for the online system and identified the types of printed products required. Functions for the effective processing of management information, as well as bibliographic data, were explicitly included. It was also apparent that there was adequate record size to meet almost all archival description and access needs, including lengthy content and historical notes and numerous access points. There was general agreement that, with minor modifications, the capabilities specified in the functional requirements report would be provided.

During the course of the year, system programming went on at RLG, and testing began in the fall. Project staff met two more times in 1983. System development was reviewed, and the specifics of implementation, training sessions, and system standards were discussed. The other major focus of discussion was the development of cooperative cataloging procedures and standards. It was well-understood by project participants that the adoption of common authority standards and cataloging conventions was critical to their realizing many of the potential benefits of network participation. Actual system use by project libraries began in January 1984. By the end of the year, eighteen institutions were using the system, and some 9,000 AMC records had been entered.

An RLIN Archival Control record is composed of two parts, a "bibliographic control" segment for recording bibliographic information and an "archival control" segment for recording management information. The archival control segment includes a "processing control" structure, which includes accessioning, donor, and location information, and an "action" structure where particular archival management functions can be specified. Multiple processing control structures can be included in a single record to record additions to existing collections received over a period of time.[19] Multiple "actions" may also be recorded relative to any particular accession. Access to "processing control" and "action" data can be restricted to only the creating repository by the use of display permits. Donor information is restricted in every case.

Along with the creation and maintenance of cataloging records, RLIN provides rich and flexible searching capabilities. Records in the AMC file are accessible through general and local indexes. Local indexes will retrieve only records belonging to the repository which created them. General indexes will search personal names, corporate names, titles, subjects, subject subdivisions (geographic, chronological, or topical), form and genre, related titles, and NUCMC number, as well as RLIN identification number (a number assigned by the system to the record). The development of a "form and genre" index was in response to the need by archivists to identify material by document type. This index allows archivists to identify all collections containing documents of a particular form, e.g., those collections containing account books or those collections containing maps. It can also be used in conjunction with a subject search, e.g., allowing a researcher to identify all collections containing Civil War diaries.[20] The "related title" index allows the retrieval of records for materials that are component parts or subunits of a particular "host" or "parent" collection. Within the repository there are also several local searches possible. They include collection number, accession number (or other local number), and donor name.

The system provides Boolean search capabilities; that is, searches can be combined, expanded, or limited using "and," "or," or "not," both within a given index or between indexes. In addition, an existing search can be modified using the term "also" and a library identifier (a four-character code which will limit the search to the holdings of a particular repository), a specific date or range of dates, repositories located in a particular state, language, or generation of microform.

The RLIN AMC file provides four different online display formats. If a search identifies more than one record, the system provides a "multiple" display. If the listing of search results will fill more than one screen, the user is first provided with the number of records retrieved. This allows the user to choose to further limit the search before viewing a lengthy listing. The "multiple" display provides limited information, including main entry (creator), title, dates, RLIN identification number, repository, and collection number. A user may then request a more detailed display. The "long" display provides a substantial amount of information in an easily-understood format, appearing very much like a traditional catalog card. In addition to main entry, title, dates, and quantity information, it provides an historical note, a narrative description of the collection, a note concerning restrictions on access or use, and a note about finding aids. The "long" display also specifies how the collection should be cited and lists all index terms that have been used in the record. The "partial" display, used mainly for technical services purposes at the creating repository, provides minimum bibliographic information and a summary of the management information. Finally, there is a "full" display available, which presents the complete record with all MARC field tags in the form in which the data was entered.

RLIN AMC can provide access to the diverse range of materials housed in a single archival repository; it can also provide access to related collections housed in repositories across the country. Additionally, within a given research library, a single search can provide access to the broad range of related sources, published and unpublished, within the library. A common search strategy could disclose musical scores created by a composer, books by or about him, and his letters and diaries. This is particularly important in libraries where descriptions of archival holdings, as well as other special collections, have traditionally been excluded from the union catalog.[21]

RLIN IMPLEMENTATION AND NATIONAL DEVELOPMENT

To facilitate system implementation and to foster the development of a national archival information data base, an RLG Archives and Manuscripts Task Force, chaired by H. Thomas Hickerson of Cornell University, was established in July 1983. An important element in the charge to the Task Force was the recommendation of acceptable bibliographic standards for archival control records. The standard adopted for RLIN AMC use is intended to encourage comprehensive cataloging of repository holdings and to facilitate system use for accessioning and records management, as well as for cataloging and reference services. The basic elements of the standard are:

1. the inclusion of a limited number of required fields in the online creation of an archival control record;
2. the application of descriptive cataloging based on *Archives, Personal Papers, and Manuscripts: A Cataloging Manual for Archival Repositories, Historical Societies, and Manuscript Libraries* (1983);[22]
3. the use of AACR2 (*Anglo-American Cataloging Rules*, 2nd ed., 1978) and the LC Name Authority File to establish the form of personal and corporate names;
4. the inclusion, when topical subject headings are used in a record, of at least one heading based on the terms and practices of *Library of Congress Subject Headings*.[23]

This standard reflects the intent of system designers to promote three levels of access integration, including access to the diverse range of holdings within a single repository, the broad spectrum of information sources within the modern research library, and the wealth of primary source documentation in the nation's archival repositories.

The Task Force has also been concerned with the enhancement of the data base through the expansion of system use and also by the conversion of existing machine-readable archival data bases and the addition of NUCMC cataloging data. The number of library repositories using the system has steadily grown, and the initial use of RLIN AMC by a state archival program began in the fall of 1984 at the State Historical Society of Wisconsin. The National Archives and Records Administration has recently announced a pilot implementation of RLIN AMC to test its suitability for controlling federal records throughout their life cycle and for improving access to those records. The data base will also be enhanced by the conversion of machine-readable records generated by the use of SPINDEX (Selective Permutation INDEXing) software. These include records of the State Historical Society of Wisconsin and also include over 10,000 records for the holdings of some 700 repositories in the state of New York. These records have resulted from the survey work of the New York Historical Resources Center at Cornell University. As additional repositories are surveyed, records will be entered directly into RLIN, generating a statewide data base. Currently, staff at Yale and Cornell Universities are conducting tests to ascertain the resources necessary to incorporate NUCMC data into the RLIN data base.

The opportunities resulting from the growing use of RLIN are being further expanded by other local and national developments. In addition to the RLG implementation, uses of the new format include those by the Historical Department of the Church of Jesus Christ of Latter-Day Saints, the Smithsonian Institution, the Chicago Historical Society, and OCLC, the largest national bibliographic utility, which implemented the new format in November 1984.[24] Other developments include the preparation by the staff of the New York State Archives of a functional requirements statement for developing enhancements to LS 2000, a local library system being marketed nationally by OCLC. Research and development are currently underway at Michigan State University on the design of a MARC application for archival management, to be implemented on a microcomputer.

Although these applications vary in both their scope and their objectives, there is no doubt that bibliographic access to archival sources will expand rapidly in the next few years. The effect on reference services will be substantial. Increasingly, researchers will have the ability to access information regarding archival holdings at sites remote from the reading rooms of archives and manuscript repositories. In many cases, access will take place in the general reference areas of research libraries. This will necessitate a broadened knowledge by reference librarians of the nature of archival materials and their use. Among network participants, it will be necessary to develop cooperative protocols for reference and interlibrary services. In order to take full advantage of these expanding opportunities, librarians and archivists must develop a heightened sense of common purpose in providing access to the wealth of resources available in the nation's archives and manuscript repositories.

FOOTNOTES

1. Theodore C. Blegen, *Grass Roots History* (Minneapolis, Minnesota: University of Minnesota Press, 1947), 253-254.
2. U.S., Library of Congress, Automated Systems Office, *MARC Formats for Bibliographic Data*, Update No. 10 (Washington, D.C.: Library of Congress, 1984).
3. "Minutes of the Meeting of the Council of the American Historical Association, December 26, 1946," *American Historical Review*, 52:3 (April 1947), 626-628.
4. Howard H. Peckham, "Manuscript Repositories and the National Register," *American Archivist*, 17:4 (October 1954), 319.
5. "Report of the Joint Committee on Historical Manuscripts," *American Archivist*, 15:2 (April 1952), 176-180.
6. Robert H. Land, "The National Union Catalog of Manuscript Collections," *American Archivist*, 17:3 (July 1954), 198-204.
7. U.S., Library of Congress, *National Union Catalog of Manuscript Collections, 1959-1961* (Ann Arbor, Michigan: J. W. Edwards, 1962), v-vi.
8. U.S., Library of Congress, Processing Services, *National Union Catalog of Manuscript Collections, Catalog, 1982* (Washington, D.C.: Library of Congress, 1983), iii.
9. Philip M. Hamer, ed., *A Guide to Archives and Manuscripts in the United States* (New Haven, Conn.: Yale University Press, 1961).
10. U.S., National Historical Publications and Records Commission, *Directory of Archives and Manuscript Repositories in the United States* (Washington, D.C.: National Archives and Records Service, 1978).
11. H. Thomas Hickerson, Joan Winters, and Venetia Beale, *SPINDEX II at Cornell University and a Review of Archival Automation in the United States* (Ithaca, New York: Department of Manuscripts and University Archives, Cornell University Libraries, 1976), 26-34.
12. Larry J. Hackman, Nancy Sahli and Dennis A. Burton, "The NHPRC and a Guide to Manuscript and Archival Materials in the United States," *American Archivist*, 40:2 (April 1977), 201-205.
13. "Minutes of the Meeting of the Council of the Society of American Archivists, October 6, 1977," *American Archivist*, 41:1 (January 1978), 119-120.
14. Elaine D. Engst, "Standard Elements for the Description of Archives and Manuscript Collections," An unpublished report to the Society of American Archivists Task Force on National Information Systems, 1980.
15. U.S., Library of Congress, MARC Development Office, *Manuscripts: A MARC Format* (Washington, D.C.: Library of Congress, 1973).
16. H. Thomas Hickerson, "Archival Information Exchange: Developing Compatibility," *Academic Libraries: Myths and Realities, Proceedings of the Third National Conference of the Association of College and Research Libraries*, ed. Suzanne C. Dodson and Gary L. Menges (Chicago: Association of College and Research Libraries, 1984), 62-66.
17. Research Libraries Group, Inc., *RLIN Archival Control Manual* (Stanford, California: Research Libraries Group, Inc., 1984).
18. Lofton Abrams, "Yale, Cornell, and Stanford Awarded Grant for Development of RLG Automated Bibliographic System for Manuscripts and Archives," *American Archivist* 46:4 (Fall, 1983), 477-480.
19. In this description of RLIN AMC capabilities, the term "collection(s)" is used to represent both manuscript collections and also archival record groups, series, and subseries (bibliographic units common in the control of governmental and institutional archives). Both the MARC format and RLIN AMC provide for the control of archival materials at any level of specificity and also allow for the cataloging of individual documents.
20. To facilitate use of form and genre information, RLG has issued a list of document types for use in field 655 (Genre/Form) of the USMARC Format for Archival and Manuscripts Control, Thomas Hickerson and Elaine Engst, comp., *Form Terms for Archival and Manuscripts Control* (Stanford, California: Research Libraries Group, Inc., 1985).

21. Kathy Hudson, "Archives and Libraries: Exploring the Integration Process" (Paper delivered at the Annual Meeting of the Society of American Archivists, Minneapolis, Minnesota, October 7, 1983).

22. Steven L. Hensen, comp., *Archives, Personal Papers, and Manuscripts: A Cataloging Manual for Archival Repositories, Historical Societies, and Manuscript Libraries* (Washington, D.C.: Library of Congress, 1983).

23. Research Libraries Group, Inc., *RLG Standard for Archives and Manuscripts in RLIN* (Stanford, California: Research Libraries Group, Inc., 1984).

24. OCLC Online Computer Library Center, Inc., *Online Systems, Archives and Manuscript Control Format* (Dublin, Ohio: OCLC, 1984).

FORTHCOMING IN THE REFERENCE LIBRARIAN

PERSONNEL ISSUES IN REFERENCE SERVICES

The Current Trends and Controversies in the Literature of Reference Services and Their Implications for the Practice of Reference Work . . . . . Carl F. Orgren and James Rice
Selecting, Training and Retaining Staff for the Library's Public Service Desks . . . . . Carol Lee Anderson
Choosing How to Staff the Reference Desk . . . . . John Montag
End User Searching: The Beginning of the End? . . . . . Geraldene Walker
Staff Sharing: A Development Program . . . . . Joan W. Jensen
The Reference Librarian in the Small Information Center: Selection and Training . . . . . Miriam H. Tees
The Reference Librarian as Personnel Administrator . . . . . William Miller
Evaluating the Reference Librarian . . . . . Sara B. Sluss
Time Management for Information Services . . . . . Bill Bailey
Role of the Manager in Reference Staff Development . . . . . Margaret Hendley
Quality Control of Reference Service in Branch Libraries of a Multi-Campus College . . . . . Pamela L. Wonsek
Everybody Needs Information . . . . . Miles Jackson
Multiple Roles of Academic Reference Librarians: Problems of Education and Training . . . . . Barbara E. Kemp
The Recruitment, Selection and Retention of Academic Reference Librarians . . . . . Ilene F. Rockman

Reference Librarians as Teachers: Ego, Ideal and Reality in a Reference Department . . . . . Ellen Broidy
Microcomputer Continuing Education Training Will Assist Reference Librarians . . . . . Thomas E. Alford
Empirical Indications for Choosing Reference Librarianship as a Profession: A Biographical Approach . . . . . Martin H. Sable
Definitions Help . . . . . Lora Landers
Selecting Reference Librarians—Signs to Look for in Selection . . . Mabel Shaw and Susan S. Whittle

For Product Safety Concerns and Information please contact our EU
representative GPSR@taylorandfrancis.com
Taylor & Francis Verlag GmbH, Kaufingerstraße 24, 80331 München, Germany

www.ingramcontent.com/pod-product-compliance
Lightning Source LLC
Chambersburg PA
CBHW052110300426
44116CB00010B/1614